Children's Friendships in Culturally Diverse Classrooms

The World of Childhood and Adolescence

Series Editor: Malcolm Clarkson,
Falmer Press Ltd
4 John Street
London

Children's Friendships in Culturally Diverse Classrooms

James G. Deegan

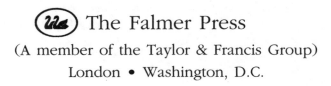 The Falmer Press

(A member of the Taylor & Francis Group)
London • Washington, D.C.

UK   The Falmer Press, 1 Gunpowder Square, London, EC4A 3DE
USA   The Falmer Press, Taylor & Francis Inc., 1900 Frost Road, Suite 101, Bristol, PA 19007

© J. Deegan 1996

First published in 1996

A catalogue record for this book is available from the British Library

Library of Congress Cataloging-in-Publication Data are available on request

ISBN 0 7507 0266 4 cased
ISBN 0 7507 0267 2 paper

Jacket design by Caroline Archer

Typeset in 10 on 12pt Garamond by
Graphicraft Typesetters Ltd., Hong Kong.

Printed in Great Britain by Biddles Ltd., Guildford and King's Lynn on paper which has a specified pH value on final paper manufacture of not less than 7.5 and is therefore 'acid free'.

Contents

Dedication

I dedicate the time and effort invested in this volume to my wife Ber, our children Conor and Ciara, and my parents Mona and Gerry.

List of Figures and Tables

Acknowledgments

I am indebted to a number of 'good listeners' from diverse places and different times for their insights, encouragement, and support. I begin by thanking the children in the classrooms and schools represented in this book for sharing the wonder of their lives with me. My thanks go especially to Jonathan, Lena, and Donna from 'Stanley Hazel Elementary School' in Atlanta, Georgia.

I am also indebted to those who have interactively spiked my inspiration in witting and unwitting ways. This small coterie provided intellectual generosity and grace and clarity of thought at critical moments in my life. These teachers inspired me to reach for self-determined levels of excellence that I did not believe were possible: Brendan Bradshaw, Lawrence Fagan, Gary Fine, John Furlong, Joan Fry, Ivor Goodson, Linda Grant, Brenda Manning, Genelle Morain, Donal Mulcahy, Tony Pellegrini, George Stanic, and Steve White.

I am thankful to my friends and colleagues in the 'Survivors Club,' Duncan Waite, Penny Oldfather, and Martha Allexsaht-Snider, for their reliable and valid friendship at all times. I am especially grateful to Martha for being such a wonderful friend and colleague, and for so often providing the critical second inspiration in my thinking on children's lives 'at promise' in culturally diverse schools and classrooms.

I am indebted to Stephanie Bales, Audrey Courtney, Kara Rebitch, and Judy Harper who typed various portions of the original manuscript. It helped a lot to be able to rely on your individual and collective expertise during the long hot summer when I was nearing my deadline.

I also thank my parents, Mona and Gerry, my brother, Michael, my extended family, and old friends in Limerick and Cork for their encouragement and pride in my professional achievements over the years. Their support is interwoven in this work. Warm thanks to our children, Conor and Ciara, for just being kids and bringing their special spark to our lives. And finally, I thank my wife, Ber, a true kindred spirit, and one who knows what it takes to be the best of friends.

I thank the editors and publishers who have published my work, and who have granted their permission to reproduce it for this volume. A special thanks goes to Malcolm Clarkson of Falmer Press for his wit and patience during the writing process.

Acknowledgments

Thanks also to:

The National Middle School Association and the *Middle School Journal* for material in Chapter 1. This was first published as DEEGAN, J.G. (1992) 'Understanding vulnerable friendships in fifth-grade culturally diverse classrooms,' *Middle School Journal*, **23**, (4) pp. 20–5.

SUNY Press for material in Chapter 2. This was first published as DEEGAN, J.G. and PELLEGRINI, A.D. (1994) 'Play and trajectories for social origins of cognition,' in BOGUE, R. and SPARIOSU, M. (eds) *The Play of the Self*, (pp. 113–35), New York, SUNY Press.

The Association for Childhood Education International and the *Journal of Research in Childhood Education* for material in Chapter 3. This was first published as DEEGAN, J.G. (1993) 'Children's friendships in culturally diverse classrooms,' *Journal of Research in Childhood Education*, **7**, (3) pp. 91–101.

The American Anthropological Association and *Anthropology and Education Quarterly* for material in Chapter 4. This was first published as DEEGAN, J.G. (1995) 'The friendly cultural stranger as self-critical reflexive narrator,' *Anthropology and Education Quarterly*, **26**, (3) pp. 1–9.

Chapter 1

Introduction: The Promise of Children's Friendships in Culturally Diverse Classrooms

It is just a few short years from the promiscuity of the sandbox to the tormented possessive feelings of a fifth grader who has just learned that his best friend and only friend is playing at another classmate's house after school. There maybe worse betrayals in store but none more influential than the sudden fickleness of an elementary school friend who has dropped us for someone more popular after all our careful, patient wooing. (Lopate, 1993, p. 79)

The world of children's friendships is always under our feet; it can be heard, if we care to listen, in most homes that have children and in the parks and schoolyards where children play. This world is commonplace but it largely goes unnoticed by most adults. (Ginsberg, Gottman, and Parker, 1986, p. 3)

To be and have friends is a fundamental human interest and concern. The traditional refrain that 'schooldays are the happiest days of our lives,' as Woods (1990) argues, frequently owes more to the joys of being and having friends than it does to the pleasures and rewards of academic learning. Yet, ironically, it is this popular perception that frequently obscures the promise of children's friendships as motivational contexts for social learning in the present culture of schools and classrooms. Why children's friendships should be an important topic of scientific investigation has a long history in psychological studies of children's early social experiences (see Hartup, 1983), and a comparatively more recent history in sociological studies of childhood (Ambert, 1986; Corsaro, 1985, 1994; Corsaro and Eder, 1990; Denzin, 1977; James and Prout, 1990; Mayall, 1994).

The importance of children's friendships has been rehearsed in late nineteenth- and early twentieth-century speculative writings on the effects of social groups on human behavior by writers such as Thomas Horton Cooley, Sigmund Freud, Emile Durkheim, Jean Piaget, and George Herbert Mead (see Renshaw, 1981). In the 1930s, Lewin's seminal field-experimentalist approach for identifying the determinants of social interaction (Lewin and Lippitt, 1938; Lewin, Lippitt, and White, 1939) firmly established 'dominant and dominating'

(James and Prout, 1990, p. 10) developmental trajectories in the research on children's peer cultures. This dominance has endured, admittedly to a lesser extent, up to the present day.

The dominant developmental framework has been heavily influenced by the Piagetian inheritance on children's social cognition. Piaget's 'genetic epistemology' links 'the biological facts of immaturity, such as dependence, to social aspects of childhood,' 'the universality of social practices surrounding childhood,' and 'the assumed naturalness of childhood' (James and Prout, 1990, p. 10). The importance of children's friendships has been conceptualized in terms of the immediate and enduring 'functions' of friendships throughout the developmental lifespan. Examples of the functions that friendships serve in childhood include 'the positive, promotive influences of general peer interaction on children's current and long-term adjustment and maturity' (see Ginsberg, Gottman, and Parker, 1986, p. 5). More specifically, Gottman, Ginsberg, and Parker (1986) state that the following six functions are evident in the developmental research on children's friendships and friendship expectations: companionship, stimulation, physical support, ego support/enhancement, social comparison, and intimacy/affection (pp. 6–11).

In complement and counterpoint to the dominant developmental trajectory, an expanding corpus of ethnographic studies on a wide array of interactive processes in children's peer cultures has gradually begun to emerge in the last quarter century (see Corsaro and Eder, 1990). This corpus includes the emergent integral strand of children's friendships in culturally diverse contexts.

Corsaro and Eder (1990) situate children's friendships within children's broader social participation experiences in their peer cultures. More specifically, they describe children's friendships as highly developed instances of the integrative functions of: *sharing* an activity, often signalled with the phrase 'We're friends, right?;' *communal* sharing in 'jump rope' games (Goodwin, 1985); and 'trading and bargaining' (Mishler, 1979) in children's early childhood education settings. Indeed, Corsaro and Eder (1990) cite Katriel's (1987) study of *ritualized* sharing among Israeli children as an exemplar of the delicate nature of negotiation in children's peer cultures. Yet, we have few studies of this kind. We need more studies that challenge the particularistic and universalistic claims of researchers from different traditions who have studied children's friendships in the past. One area that needs to be more fully investigated is children's 'own' perspectives on their friendships, and how their developing constructions of friendship become embedded in their social lives in culturally diverse classrooms.

The present work owes much to recent ethnographic studies of children's friendships in mainstream (Fine, 1987; Pollard, 1985; Rizzo, 1989), and culturally diverse pre-school and elementary school classrooms (Corsaro, 1994; Davies, 1982; Grant, 1984; Schofield, 1981, 1982; Sleeter and Grant, 1986; Troyna and Hatcher, 1992). This book will include a range of recent research literature from psychology, anthropology, and sociology on children's friendships from nursery school through middle school, with underrepresented sociological theories of childhood and children serving as the prismatic lens for description and interpretation. A specific focus of the book will be on early adolescence and the grade levels in upper elementary school and lower middle school that approximate this highly emotional transitional phase in children's social lives.

Although some significant emergent studies have begun to challenge existing theoretical and conceptual orthodoxies, the research on children's friendships in culturally diverse classrooms is still very much in the formative stages. Two notable challenges will be discussed in greater detail in Chapter 3. One study is Corsaro's (1994) comparative study of children's deeply embedded collective and interpretive reproduction friendship processes in three early childhood education settings (an Italian scuola materna, a Head Start Program, and a private nursery school in the United States). The other study is Troyna's and Hatcher's (1992) study of the part that race and friendships played as plausible explanatory frameworks for incidents in children's everyday lives in mainly white primary schools in Britain.

In recent years, the challenges of teaching and learning about children's friendships has been closely related to multicultural and social reconstructionist approaches for developing interpersonal awareness, minimizing stereotypes and stereotyping, expressing personal feelings, promoting individual uniqueness and worth, and encouraging cross-group communication (Grant and Sleeter, 1989). There is, however, a lack of congruence between existing theory, emerging research, and popular action-based curricula aimed at fostering positive aspects of children's friendships in culturally diverse schools and classrooms. I will argue throughout this book that children's friendships deserve closer investigation because they are central to children's social lives, influence the way children negotiate social participation, conflict, and adult rules and authority (Corsaro and Eder, 1990). It will also be argued that if we are to accurately reflect the realities of children's friendships, then we need to systematically examine friendships in culturally diverse classrooms as complex phenomena that can potentially influence a wide range of classroom instructional and non-instructional processes. Simply, we need to discover the basic friendship processes at work in today's continually changing classrooms.

Three Popular Misconceptions

What we typically understand as children's friendships are commonplace phenomena that suffer from a number of popular misconceptions. Three illustrative examples are discussed here. One misconception relates to the fact that since friendship has been the topic of popular and academic attention for more than 2,000 years (Aries, 1962), there is little left to say about it. Indeed, the ancient Greeks are responsible for a number of unexhausted questions concerning friendships including 'whether friendship is intrinsically singular and exclusive or plural and democratic . . .' (p. 80). While it is true, as Lopate (1993) remarked, that great essayists such as Aristotle and Cicero, Seneca and Montaigne, Francis Bacon and Samuel Johnson, William Hazlitt, Ralph Waldo

Emerson, and Charles Lamb, among several others, have all 'taken their crack at it' (p. 78), we need to look beyond the legacy of the great classical thinkers.

Additionally, simply juxtaposing classical perspectives on adult friendships with children's developing understandings of friendships needs to be weighed judiciously. Such approaches tend to define friendships as highly developed interpersonal constructs, with little respect for children's friendships as socially constructed processes. This is especially acute when discussing developmental and diversity themes.

In her recent book, *The Challenge to Care in Schools: An Alternative Approach to Education* (1992), Noddings provides an example of how the main criterion of friends wishing friends well 'for their own sake' (p. 98), which has been elaborated in Aristotelian *Nicomachean Ethics*, can provide a referent for caring in schools, while not minimizing the centrality of children in the challenge to care. Indeed, there is renewed interest in questions concerning 'tensions' between moral requirements and friendships (see Noddings, 1992; Edgerton, 1993). This topic has engaged the minds of Jean Piaget and Lawrence Kohlberg, among many others, earlier in the century. Put simply, the question that is often posed runs as follows: 'When should moral requirements outweigh the demands of friendship?' This is an inherent question in the discourse on children's friendship, but one that needs more comprehensive examination than will be provided within the scope of this book. The routine privileging of adult perspectives on children's friendships, however, will be discussed again with reference to popular misconceptions about friendships later in this chapter.

Leading contemporary popular writers such as Roald Dahl, Tracy Kidder, and Stephen King have succeeded admirably in combining the literary and social domains of reality in their writings on children's friendships. Indeed many of us will have observed 10-year-old girls who have been inspired by the heroines's phrase of 'kindred spirits' in Montgomery's book, *Anne of Green Gables* (1944). Other readers will have observed generations of 10-year-old boys digging side by side with 'raging desire' for hidden treasure like Huck Finn and Tom Sawyer in Twain's book, *Adventures of Huckleberry Finn* (1995 [1884]). Indeed, much has been written in recent literary discourse on the morality of Huck's struggle between the principle that demands he return the slave Jim, or break the principle and go to hell rather than turn on his friend (see Boostrom, 1994). But accounts such as these, which extend back to Antigone and Sophocles and forward to Spock and Kirk, notwithstanding their common-sense resonances, are essentially fictions.

Kidder's book, *Among Schoolchildren* (1989) is noteworthy because it represents a potent example of the complementarity inherent in literary and social domains of children's friendships in culturally diverse contexts. Although Kidder acknowledges the influences of histories of education (for example, Bowles and Gintis, 1976), sociological studies of teaching (for example, Jackson, 1968), and critiques of education (for example, Kozol, 1967), his approach is undeniably fueled from the literary vantage point. Quite simply, we need to complement the rich lineage of literary accounts of children's friendships with sociological studies of children's friendship activities, routines, rituals, concerns, and values as motivational contexts for learning in today's culturally diverse classrooms. The challenge of combining literary and ethnographic accounts of friendships will be addressed in Chapter 5.

A second misconception relates to the fact that adults always know best when it comes to children's friendships. This misconception privileges adult perspectives above what children often understand and act upon in their own friendships. It is especially relevant when it comes to the selection of children's friendships. Although teacher–parent conferences typically follow scripted conversations focused on academic learning and progress, there are also those counter-intuitive moments when we get around to asking, 'How's Johnny doing socially?,' 'Has Janie any friends?,' or 'Is Tony a good "mixer"?' Something twigs and we remember that, in addition to learning how to do complicated long division problems, friends continue to play key roles in what are often our most memorable positive and negative social learning experiences in school.

Sometimes it also registers that our own end-of-year fifth-grade class photograph with its pattern of relative 'sameness' looks a lot a different from our own child's class photograph in today's fifth-grade classroom. Whatever the significance of those garish bell-bottom trousers, leg-of-mutton sleeves, and Peter Pan collars as social status symbols, today, there is more to both sets of photographs than immediately meets the eye. There are 'stories' of friendships created, sustained, and broken in both photographs. Whether we actively or benignly address the potential of everyday situations like this, when the child within us and the child beside us confront each other, is part of the message in this book.

A third misconception relates to the fact that children's friendships are often perceived as 'common-sense' social constructions. While there is much to be said for the wise use of common-sense knowledge, we need to more systematically examine the routines, rituals, activities and values of children's social lives as dynamic processes and not as calcified ones. A common difficulty that some adults experience when addressing children's friendships is their chameleon-like nature—they are highly colorful, elusive, and unpredictable phenomena. They are close but distant, more the stuff of anecdote than interpretation, and typically take place in the hurly-burly of playgrounds, lunchrooms, and around school hallways. They are often silent, detached, and invisible phenomena for some adults who stand in their midst everyday. I will suggest ways for negotiating involvement and detachment when addressing children's friendships with diverse social groups in Chapters 4, 5, and 7.

Clearly, our operationalized understandings of children's friendships both wittingly and unwittingly affect our selection of a wide range of instructional, management, and curricular decision-making processes (Deegan, 1993). I will argue that children's friendships are full of 'promise', potentially robust, sophisticated social constructions, and that there is a place for adults in fostering positive learning environments for the development of children's friendships.

Children's Friendships 'At Promise'

Beneath the benign appearances of children's friendships lies a conceit. The path of friendship is fraught with 'betrayals,' 'sudden fickleness,' and failed 'wooings.' The parameters of harmony and hostility undergird the continuous negotiation of the 'codes' of children's lore, language, and friendships (Corsaro, 1985; Davies, 1984; Fine, 1987; Opie and Opie, 1959 and 1969; Pollard, 1985). In similar vein to Swadener and Lubeck's (1995) work on deconstructing the discourse of 'risk,' I suggest that we need to begin to utilize the construct of friendships 'at promise' to convey that *all* children's friendships can potentially become motivational contexts for useful learning in our end-of-the-twentieth-century world. Throughout this book, the conceptual understanding of friendships 'at promise' will be used interchangeably with syntactical derivatives such as 'promise,' 'promises,' and 'promising.' The challenge of understanding the 'promise' of children's friendships is the touchstone for this book.

This is not a book of 'success stories' but one about potential success stories. My approach is tempered by the realization that children's friendships include many children's versions of the negotiation and struggle towards equality and harmony. This approach suggests that children negotiate their friendships against backcloths of unique and contingent 'mixes' of contextual dissonances related to race, ethnicity, gender, class, community, disability, and an array of continually changing life-situational, sociocultural factors. In this book, I pose a set of 'interrogatives' which are intended to stimulate interrelatedness between my theoretical observations and data drawn from fieldwork and interviews in the following chapters.

The following basic interpretive question fueled my interests and concerns from the outset: Why is this friendship_____(routine, ritual, activity, interest, concern, value) the way it is and not different? (see Erickson, 1984, p. 62). My intent was to remain aware of 'the commonsense and taken-for-granted knowledge of the participants, and to suggest analytical concepts by which such tacit knowledge can be named and made available for reflection' (Pollard, 1985, p. xi). The following questions build on Swadener and Lubeck's (1995) set of 'interrogatives,' and are aimed at challenging cultural deprivation deficit models and contributing to the emergent discourse on children 'at promise' in current educational discourse. These 'layered' questions will be addressed in different ways, and at different junctures, in the next seven chapters:

1. Who has 'promising' friendships in culturally diverse classrooms?
2. Why are these friendships 'promising'?
3. Who defines children's friendships? How have the criteria for or definitions of friendships changed? What are the differences between children's friendships and their broader social participation experiences in their peer cultures?
4. What is the 'etiology' of the concept of children's friendships 'at promise'? How is the emergent discourse one of 'promise,' 'negotiation,' and

'nonsychrony.' What are some of the complexities in the discourse of 'promise'? In what ways does the concept of 'promise' reconcile tensions between harmony and conflict in children's friendships in culturally diverse classrooms?

5. To what extent does the emergent discourse of 'promise' challenge 'common-sense and taken-for-granted knowledge' about friendships? What sensitizing reflexive techniques are useful when studying children's 'promising' friendships in culturally diverse classrooms?

6. In what ways is the discourse of 'promise' different from essentialist, reductionist, and dogmatic cultural deprivation deficit approaches to children's friendships? What is the connection between nonsynchronous or contradictory explanations of race, class, gender, or any other sociocultural variable in the classroom locality and the emergent discourse of children's 'promising' friendships?

7. How are those of us who work with children in culturally diverse classrooms making sense of involvement and detachment as a dualism or a duality when we are among children's friendships?

8. What inquiry approaches could be developed by teachers for understanding 'promising' friendships in culturally diverse classrooms? To what extent could student teachers begin inquiring into the unique and contingent dynamics of children's friendships in their field placements?

9. What connections exist between emergent insights on 'promising' friendships and curricular decisions related to culturally-sensitive teaching and learning approaches?

10. How might emergent insights on children's 'promising' friendships inform policy, pedagogy, and teacher preparation. What are the specific challenges for educational renewal and development in school–university partnerships?

Through a Lens Harshly and Softly

Peacock's (1986) photographic metaphors of 'harsh light' and 'soft focus' provide a useful lens for reading the chapters on the ethnographic contexts, perspectives, and voices of children's friendships in culturally diverse classrooms in this book. Peacock's metaphors describe a worldview that consists of two elements. One is a concern with the basic reality of the human condition, free of cultural influence; the other is a broadly based holism that attempts to grasp all aspects of that condition, including its relation to the self-critical reflexive researcher. These lenses are intended as a caution against the rhetoric of essentialist, reductionist, and dogmatic notions of race and inequality focused on biological explanations of education (see, for example, Dunn, 1987; Jensen, 1984). This rhetoric has a tendency to reduce children's friendships to outcome phenomena or proximal variables (McCarthy, 1990). These outcome or proximal notions also have the potential for conceptualizing children's friendships in terms of stereotypical patterns of inclusion and exclusion based on cognitive, linguistic, and scholastic development.

Within the warps and wefts of the stories reported in this book lies a forceful reminder that contextual dissonances in children's friendships are not always a matter of far away drums and battles long since won. These stories reveal compelling evidence for the immediate concerns and issues of children's friendships in culturally diverse classrooms. In Chapters 2 and 3, selected prominent psychological, anthropological, sociological, and educational accounts of children's friendships are overviewed and focused with reference to the challenges for cross-disciplinary research trajectories on the topic of friendships. Cast another way, these accounts reflect children's everyday friendship routines, rituals, activities, interests, concerns, and values, and provide approximations of how these features become embedded in children's meanings of cultural diversity. Readers will discover chapters that not only challenge some of the 'elaborated ideologies' of race, ethnicity, class, gender, and community, but also hear the voices of those for whom Paul Simon sings as whispered in 'the wells of silence.'

Among the voices from the wells of silence that cast fresh and revealing light on cultural diversity are those of Lena, Jonathan, and Donna, whose thwarted efforts to sustain their friendships in the face of contextual dissonances is discussed in Chapter 4. There is also my 'own' voice 'retelling tales' of my attempts to make sense of my presence as a friendly cultural stranger in a study of children's friendships in a culturally diverse fifth-grade classroom in Chapter 5. In Chapter 6, I introduce an inquiry approach for learning about research and teaching about research on children's friendships in an early childhood education teacher education component of a school-university partnership, currently underway at The University of Georgia, and in local area public elementary schools. In Chapter 7, two student teachers, Meredith Gaskill and Ben Lauricella, tell their beginning stories of personal and professional experiences studying children's friendships, and the 'lessons' they learned which will influence their own future research and practice in culturally diverse classrooms. In Chapter 8, I attempt to link thematic trajectories for curriculum reform and renewal, and conclude on an optimistic note.

Throughout the following chapters, I will speak as a writer with research interests and concerns in children's social lives as complex and profound phenomena. I will also speak as a father whose oldest child is currently leaving the safety and security of sandbox culture for the complex social realties of a local elementary school, and whose second child is being introduced to the local sandbox culture for the first time. And finally I will speak as a former primary schoolteacher in the Irish national school system who often lapses into the long dream back to Ireland.

Chapter 2

Theoretical Foundations of Children's Friendships in Culturally Diverse Classrooms

... there does not exist, nor has there ever existed a sociology of childhood. (Denzin, 1977, p. 1)

A theory of children's relationships has to be able to account for both friendship and hostility. It has to be able to explain both the dynamic towards equality and harmony and the dynamic towards dominance and conflict. (Troyna and Hatcher, 1992, p. 48)

In this chapter, I will examine the theoretical foundations of children's friendships in culturally diverse classrooms. I will begin by reviewing the challenges of defining friendships, broadly, noting especially the extent to which researchers have wrestled with the homogenization and marginalization of children's friendships in sociological, psychological, anthropological, and educational discourse. Then, I will discuss approaches for defining the 'friendships' and 'cultural diversity' couplet as more than one of simple and direct correspondence, noting the irreducible tensions that exist between these twin and interrelated sociocultural themes. Finally, I will address the challenges of conjunctural or middle level nonsynchronous theories of diversity, noting especially the interactive effects of such constitutive processes as 'negotiation,' 'opposition,' 'consonance and dissonance,' 'boundary,' and 'promise' inherent in recent research on children's friendships.

Dehomogenizing and Demarginalizing

One of the significant challenges facing those who study children's friendships is how to avoid the invidious trap of homogenizing friendships within children's broader social participation experiences. Many definitions of children's friendships which attempt to tease out the parameters of the phenomena abound in the relevant literature. Hartup (1983), a leading developmental psychologist, distinguished the semantic difficulties in using the word peer to denote 'equal standing.' He discussed that: (i) equivalences in chronological age does not mean equivalences in other attributes (for example, intellectual abilities, social skills, and physical beauty), and (ii) that psychologists may have overemphasized these experiences in their theories of socialization.

Some psychologists have recast Piaget's 'developmental staircase' in terms of flexible changes rather than overall transformations, and have emphasized environmental rather than chronological factors in studies of children's peer interactions (see Chance and Fischman, 1987). Developmental psychologists have contextualized children's friendships with reference to the essential conditions of reciprocity and commitment between individuals who see themselves more or less as equals in a range of developmental studies on the topic (Berndt, 1981, 1983; Bigelow, 1977; Bigelow and LaGaipa, 1975; Selman, 1980; Youniss, 1980).

In contrast to what James and Prout (1990) have described as the 'dominant and dominating' (p. 10) developmental accounts of childhood provided by psychology, sociologists have generally tended to marginalize phenomena associated with children. Ambert (1986) explained the lack of interest in sociological studies of childhood in terms of the following twinfold sociocultural situation:

1. The premium placed on certain types of knowledge by the founding fathers of sociology that emphasized macro issues and relegated the study of women and, by extension, children to a marginal concern.
2. The absence of incentives to specialize, until comparatively recently, in micro issues, such as peer interaction, learning styles, and children's friendships.

The marginalization of children in sociological studies led Denzin (1977) to remark that 'there does not exist, nor has there ever existed a sociology of childhood' (p. 1). Using a symbolic-interactionist perspective, he examined the languages of children, their socialization experiences, and the emergence of their self-conceptions within a naturalistic context. His essays attempted to probe the 'hidden, secret, and private worlds of the child and the caretaker' (p. 2). Although Denzin's contribution was, arguably, one of the pivotal turning points in attempting to problematize traditional perspectives on children's socialization, his work is marked by the implicit binarism of classical socialization theory in which the child, essentially, becomes 'social by becoming adult' (James and Prout, 1990, p. 13). Thirty years after Denzin's clarion call urging researchers to redress the chronic state of the sociology of childhood, Corsaro (1985) decried the state of sociological theory on childhood socialization as 'primitive' (p. 879), noting especially the paucity of emphases in the research on children's friendships.

While sociologists have critiqued developmental perspectives for their adherence to individualism, abstract conceptions of the states of friendships, and emphasis on the endpoints of development (Harré, 1986), they have only recently begun to examine children's friendships in the largely unexplored contexts of culturally diverse schools and classrooms (Grant, 1981, 1984; Schofield,

1981, 1982; Sleeter and Grant, 1986). In Chapter 3, I will examine emergent sociological studies of children's friendships with close reference to the tenets of what James and Prout (1990) describe as the 'emergent paradigm' of the sociology of childhood. The tenets of the paradigm are worth rehearsing here, however, because they provide a concise approximation of the salient theoretical and conceptual underpinnings for the present work:

1. Childhood is understood as a social construction. As such it provides an interpretive frame for contextualizing the early years of human life. Childhood, as distinct from biological immaturity, is neither a natural nor a universal feature of human groups but appears as a specific structural or cultural component of many societies.
2. Childhood is a variable of social analysis. It can never be entirely divorced from other variables such as class, gender, or ethnicity. Comparative and cross-cultural analysis reveals a variety of childhoods rather than a single and universal phenomenon.
3. Children's social relationships and cultures are worthy of study in their own right, independent of the perspective and concern of adults.
4. Children are and must be seen as active in the construction and determination of their own social lives, the lives of those around them, and of the societies in which they live. Children are not just the passive subjects of social structures and processes.
5. Ethnography is a particularly useful methodology for the study of childhood. It allows children a more direct voice and participation in the production of sociological data than is usually possible through experimental or survey styles of research.
6. Childhood is a phenomenon in relation to which the double hermeneutic of the social sciences is acutely present (see Giddens, 1976). That is to say, to proclaim a new paradigm of childhood sociology is also to engage in and respond to the process of reconstructing childhood in society. (Giddens, 1976, pp. 8–9)

The specific tenets of the paradigm that undergird the present work rest on the centrality of children's friendships as socially constructed, integrally woven into, but not reducible, to the effects of race, ethnicity, gender, and class, and autonomously constructed by children in their own social worlds. Finally, the present work is theoretically and conceptually consonant with the shift 'from function to meaning' (Crick, 1976, p. 2), and 'the study of social categories rather than groups' (James and Prout, 1990, p. 8) in the sociology of childhood. Illustrative examples of social categories in the research on children's friendships will be discussed in Chapters 4, 5, and 7.

The existence of so many definitions of children's friendships has created the lack of a central definition in the research on the topic. Epstein's (1983) definition of children's friendships as consisting of primary and secondary groups exemplifies the attempts of some sociologists to a provide a sensitizing definition of friendships. She described friends as voluntary associates who form a *primary group*, or clique, and peers as the larger, often involuntary population, or *secondary group* from which friends are chosen (p. 15). She also overviewed how friends have been addressed in the sociological literature in terms of:

a) *type* (for example, acquaintances, just friends, good friends, best friends);

b) *patterns of selection* (for example, reciprocated or unreciprocated choices, equal or unequal statuses);

c) *sociometric indices* (for example, popularity, friendliness, isolation, and rejection). (See Epstein, 1983, pp. 15–16).

The existence of so many definitions, and embedded definitions, aimed at describing the superordinate features of children's friendships prompts the need for a sensitizing definition that views children's friendships as conceptually problematic and has the potential to lead to fresh insights.

Defining Children's Friendships

A critical weakness in the diversity of definitions derives from the failure of researchers to conceptualize the potential of social categories in the overlap of terms. The conceptual language on children's friendships is still in the formative stages of development. As Hargreaves (1978) argued, 'tacit knowledge based on experience is rarely made explicit in studies of social relationships because of the lack of a conceptual language with which to express it' (p. xi).

In his study of Little League baseball and preadolescent culture, Fine (1981) provided a threefold conceptualization of *friendship* grounded in symbolic interactionism as 'a staging area for interaction, a cultural institution for the transmission of knowledge, and a crucible for the shaping of selves' (p. 41). This definition derives from the mainstream sociological accounts of Mead's (1934) theory of self, Goffman's (1959) dramaturgical variant, and McCall's (1970) perspectives on friendships as benign cultural institutions. This sensitizing definition, with one notable conceptual disclaimer, serves as the definition for the present work. Fine's conceptualization of children's friendships includes the following threefold operational premise:

1. *Friendship-as-a-staging area*: This highlights the fact that the presence of friends activates a social context for the performance of actions.

2. *Friendship-as-a-shaper-of-the-self*: This premise provides the nexus in which a development of the self and role flexibility can occur.

3. *Friendship-as-a-cultural-institution*: This premise emphasizes the imperative for children 'to learn the process by which social meanings are

constructed, ways of knowing the expectations of others, and methods of determining their likely actions'. (1981, p. 47)

In the present work the notion of friendships as a crucible for cultural transmission is supplanted by the notion of friendships as continually negotiated in unique and contingent situations. This distinction cuts to the heart of the multidirectionality of friendships and their recursive rather than single, parallel, or dual influences in children's social lives. It removes the tendency for objectifying friendships by placing children in the pivotal role in creating their own friendships. It also affirms children's ownership of their own friendships. The modified threefold-interactionist definition of children's friendships will be operationalized in an ethnographic study of children's friendships in a fifth-grade culturally diverse classroom in Atlanta, Georgia, in the southeastern United States in Chapter 4.

The recursive processes of children's friendships was a central focus in Corsaro and Eder's (1990) synthesis of the literature on children's peer cultures. One of the noteworthy features of their synthesis was the centrality of a variant of Gidden's (1984) structuration theory as a lens for examining children's peer cultures as autonomous and creative social systems. Corsaro and Eder (1990) acknowledge that much of the impetus for interpretive theories in education has been generated by Giddens' sociological theory of structuration, as outlined in his 'classic' work *The Constitution of Society* (1984). This work has had a catalytic effect on traditional sociological theories of structure and human agency. The essence of Gidden's structuration theory is a reconceptualization of the traditional dualism that has divided sociological theories of structure and human agency. Instead of dualism, Giddens made the case for the 'duality' of structure and human agency. To briefly elaborate, 'structure [is] the medium and outcome of the conduct it recursively organizes; the structural properties of social systems do not exist outside of the action but are chronically implicated in its production and reproduction' (Giddens, 1984, p. 374).

Recently, the influence of Giddens' structuration theory has penetrated through to the sociology of education (see Shilling, 1992). Although deriving its genesis from sociological theories of inquiry, Giddens' structuration theory has posed a strong challenge for the deterministic perspectives of dominant reproduction theories in educational discourse (for example, Bourdieu and Passeron, 1977; Bowles and Gintis, 1976). One significant outcome of this challenge has been the emergence of fresh perspectives on the themes of access to cultural resources and differential adult treatment that have traditionally been central to cultural reproduction theories of education.

Interpretive theorists have branched out into children's worlds of playmates in playgroups and nursery schools. Corsaro and Eder (1990) have elaborated a derivative of Giddens' work, described as *interpretive reproduction* (p. 200). They describe the core of interpretive reproduction as not merely what Vygotskian theorists might describe as 'internalization' of the adult world, but a process whereby 'children become part of adult culture through their negotiations with adults and their creative production of a series of peer cultures with other children' (p. 201). Corsaro's (1994) work on children's friendships in comparative early childhood education settings will be prominently situated in the research on children's friendships in Chapter 3. The salient connection with the present work lies in the shared emphasis on the negotiation of the duality of constraint and construction in structure and human agency.

Defining Cultural Diversity

The importance of children's friendships in culturally diverse contexts has immediate and enduring significance for the social well-being of children and society. Against backcloths of disturbing symbolism and age-old enmities, children are attempting to learn, work, and live together free of racial, ethnic, sexual, class, ability, religious, and community prejudice. Whether we can *all* 'get along' is one of the paradoxical challenges in modern developed countries, such as England, Australia, and the United States.

We know very little, however, of what it is like to be and have friends and how developing conceptions of friendship become embedded in children's social lives. Specifically, we are lacking studies that serve as complement and counterpoint to conventional views which stress biological and cultural deficit models. These models typically tend to undermine, for example, how children negotiate the challenges of life-situational factors such as transiency, being a runaway, and the drug culture in their social lives. Some of these challenges will be discussed in Chapter 4. We need to focus on how children 'refashion' external or life-situational influences in their own unique and contingent friendships. How children are forging friendships against significant odds is one of the foci of this book. I will argue that learning to help the children that we worry most about in our classrooms can begin with action research investigations of children's friendships in instructional and noninstructional settings. Applied action research projects focused on children's friendships will be discussed in Chapters 6 and 7.

The challenges of making connections between the heuristically separate domains of children's friendships and cultural diversity calls to mind two interrelated questions. I heard the first question articulated by Henry Trueba in his keynote address to the Qualitative Research in Education Conference on the theme of 'Cultural Diversity: Contexts, Perspectives, and Voice' in Athens, Georgia in January, 1993. With the heat and glare of the media blitz that followed the three days of rioting in the African-American ghettoes of Los Angeles in the previous late April and early May beginning to recede, Trueba asked: 'What is the nature of American diversity and the role of schools in creating an adequate learning environment in which all children can learn, work and live together, free of sexual, racial, and ethnic prejudice?'

Given the centrality of friendships in children's social lives, Trueba's question presupposes the twin and interrelated concerns of this book: To what extent do children embed their everyday meanings of friendships in the reality of their own lives, and; how can those of us who stand among children's friendships help foster a positive learning environment in which all children can build friendships together, free of sexual, racial, and ethnic prejudice? I will argue that children's friendships are integral elements in children's negotiation of the contradictory perspectives, contexts, and voices of other children from diverse legitimate cultures in today's increasingly diverse public elementary schools in Chapters 3–8.

What is meant by *cultural diversity* is largely contingent on whatever root definition of culture is preferred. Scholars generally speak about culture in terms of its meanings and characteristics. Symbolic anthropologists Spradley and McCurdy (1975) argued that early attempts to define culture were characterized by exhaustive lists of cultural features. Throughout much of this century, Tylor's (1871) definition of culture as 'that complex whole which includes knowledge, art, morals, law, custom, and any other capabilities and habits acquired by man as a member of society' (p. 11) remained the authoritative one. Kroeber and Kluckhohn (1952) derived a summary definition of culture from some 160 definitions. They emphasized the intangible, symbolic, and ideational aspects of group life as critical features of culture.

Spradley and McCurdy (1975) defined culture as 'the acquired knowledge that people use to interpret experience and to generate behavior' (p. 51). In similar vein, Spindler (1982) described *cultural knowledge* as the knowledge that participants use 'to guide their behavior in the various social settings that they find themselves in' (p. 5). Spradley and McCurdy (1975) maintained that 'because all definitions are arbitrary, it is not meaningful to ask, which definition of culture is the best one? We must inquire instead about the purpose and usefulness of any definition' (p. 41). A critical factor in the selection of an operational definition of culture for the present work rested with finding one that was consistent with Fine's (1981) threefold-interactionist definition of children's friendships, and one that clearly had the potential to lead to fresh insights on the topic.

Defining Children's Friendships in Diverse Classrooms

The definition of culture used in the present work is rooted in symbolic-interactionist theory and is intended to lead to evidence on how children construct meanings of their own friendships in *bellwether* (Goetz and LeCompte, 1984), or highly developed instances of cultural diversity in public elementary school classrooms. These cases include unique and contingent 'mixes' of racial, ethnic, gender, class, community, and other sociocultural variables in the membership composition of the classrooms described in this book. Culture is also defined 'as consisting of behavioral products, ideas that emerge through interaction, material objects made by humans, or given meaning by them, and behaviors seen as meaningful by actors and observers' (Fine, 1987, pp. 124–5).

This bellwether definition makes explicit that cultural knowledge is not the whole of culture, as Sleeter and Grant (1986) argued, but that 'it is necessary to observe the social behavior of members of a cultural group in order to identify patterns in their activities and rituals' (p. 9). There still remains the challenge of 'interrelating' more systematically the constitutive elements of children's friendships in culturally diverse classrooms.

There is a mutually reinforcing tension between the sociological constructs of children's friendships and the particular cultural milieu in which they are given meaning. The challenge is rendered all the more difficult by the fact that friendship like culture is all encompassing, yet elusive, diffusive and ultimately generative. The challenge, however, augurs well for the symbolic interactionist's interest in meaning as social, and the ethnographer's charge to reconceptualize rather than verify existing conceptualizations of the world around them. As Hargreaves (1978) has argued, ethnography in combination with symbolic interactionism can provide 'a language for speaking about that which is not normally spoken about' (p. 19).

Until recently, the literature on children's friendships in culturally diverse classrooms had developed along parallel lines of inquiry. Indicative of this parallelism was the early literature on race, gender, class, and schooling, for example, that focused on educational outcome as opposed to social processes (for a summary of the literature, see Grant, 1981). In the last twenty-five years, research on children's friendships in culturally diverse settings (Grant, 1981, 1984; Schofield, 1981, 1982; Sleeter and Grant, 1986) has emerged as a fully fledged theme in the sociology of childhood. I will review the roots and branches of the relevant literature on children's friendships in culturally diverse classrooms in Chapter 3.

Nonsynchrony, Negotiation, and Promise in Children's Friendships in Culturally Diverse Classrooms

Fortunately, there are emergent sociological theories that can potentially shed light on the diffusive and generative nature of race, ethnicity, gender, class, disability, and community on children's friendships in schools in Britain and the United States. I argue, as does McCarthy (1990), that a conjunctural or middle level theory is necessary if we are to get a better handle on the nonsynchronous or contradictory ways that children's friendships operate in schools.

In the United States, McCarthy (1990) argued against the limitations of Apple and Weiss's (1983) parallelist position when applied to institutional settings. Apple and Weiss (1983) argued that 'the unequal processes and outcomes of teaching and learning and of schooling in general are produced by constant interactions among three dynamics (race, gender, and class) and in three spheres (economic, political, and cultural)' (p. 25). McCarthy advanced an alternative framework — what he called the *contradictory* or *nonsynchronous* position. McCarthy argued that the dynamics of race, gender, and class have interactive outcomes and are systematically contradictory or nonsynchronous. These outcomes can potentially lead to an increase or decrease in the effects of race, or any other variable in local school settings.

Whenever McCarthy's concept of 'contradiction' appears in this book, the positive motivational connotation is the preferred one. McCarthy suggests that it is the 'discontinuities in majority/minority experiences in schooling that can provoke or motivate qualitative changes in social relations between blacks and whites' (1990, p. 15). Seeing the hidden potential for change in children's friendships is one of the keys to fostering positive social relations in culturally diverse classrooms.

In Britain, Troyna and Hatcher (1992) called for a theory of social relationships that has 'to be able to explain both the dynamic towards equality and harmony and dominance and conflict' (p. 48). One of the critical features of their theory focused on how children define connections between macro-micro dynamics, including social structures, ideologies, common-sense understandings, individual identities, and friendships. More specifically, they argued that all children have their own model of social network which derives from a unique and contingent 'mix' of 'elaborated ideologies,' for example, ethnicity, 'refashioned into common sense through practical experience' (p. 49), and other elements of common sense, for example, 'the implications of friendship for dominance and equality' (p. 49).

Fine's (1987) and Rosenberg's (1975) work on social context will be discussed here as examples of attempts to define the parameters of children's social relationships. Fine (1987) used the concept of *idioculture*, derived from the Greek word *idios* which means 'own,' to connote group culture based on 'a system of knowledge, beliefs, behaviors, and customs shared by members of an interacting group to which members can refer and that serve as a basis of further interaction' (p. 125). Building on Bales (1970) classic book, *Personality and Interpersonal Relations*, Fine argued that group members in Little League baseball teams drew up boundaries to maintain the goals of the group and to resist intrusion. Examples of idiocultural ways of differentiating members from outsiders included: nicknames, jokes, insults, beliefs, rules of conduct, clothing styles, songs, narratives, gestures, and recurrent fantasies. Although this conceptualization establishes some critical points regarding the goals and services provided by boundary maintenance, it leaves unanswered questions about what happens when children tend to 'hover' at the parameters, and those seldom discussed 're-entry' approaches that are based on continually changing temporal, attitudinal, and spatial factors in children's social relationships. This factor is especially critical during the fluxes of early adolescence and adolescence.

Rosenberg (1975) defined as *contextual dissonance* being a member of a minority not valued by the majority in the classroom *contextual dissonance*. His focus constitutes a different phenomenon than the 'classic' sociological ideas of *group atmosphere* (Lippitt and White, 1947), *ward atmosphere* (Caudill, 1958), *climate of opinion* (Bryce, 1916; Coleman, 1961) and *Zeitgeist*. A fundamental feature of Rosenberg's theory of dissonance is the view that 'the environment is not seen as dissonant or consonant in itself; it is only dissonant or consonant for a given individual' (1975, p. 98). Rosenberg stressed that the negative consequences of minority status within the immediate context derive from the fact that social comparison processes operate more forcefully at the face-to-face level rather than when society at large is the frame of reference. Rosenberg's theory of contextual consonance and dissonance posits that these features are 'an exact expression of the other' (p. 100). On the dissonant context of race and adolescent self-concept, Rosenberg wrote as follows:

> One situation of dissonance or consonance usually not recognized as such is racial integration or segregation. The confusion is probably due to connotations of the term involved. We tend to think of dissonance as bad but integration as good, of consonance as good but segregation as bad. Yet, technically and, as we shall see, psychologically, the one is an exact expression of the other. (p. 100)

Rosenberg's theory of dissonance is closely related to Troyna and Hatcher's (1992) argument that a valid theory of children's friendships should include the 'oppositional' dynamics of friendships. This is a topic that I will return to when I discuss how some of the specific oppositional dynamics of children's friendships were negotiated in a number of ethnographic studies in Chapter 3.

What is missing from extant theoretical frameworks is a sensitizing parameter that helps to explain how the unique and contingent 'mix' of concerns, needs, abilities, and capacities that exist in local educational contexts are negotiated in children's friendships. Quite simply, the parameters of children's friendships need to be operationalized. Cohen's (1985) sensitizing definition of *boundary* as potentially marked by, but not necessarily reducible to racial, ethnic, linguistic, or religious expressions is used in the present work. As Cohen explains, boundaries 'may be thought of as existing in the minds of their beholders' (p. 12), where they 'may be perceived in rather different terms not only by people on opposite sides of it, but by people on the same side' (p. 12). This operational use of boundary incorporates some of the symbolic referents in Fine's (1987) concept of idioculture, while encompassing the potential for contradictory patterns related to diverse sociocultural factors in McCarthy's (1990) nonsynchronous theory of race and social inequality.

Conclusion

In this chapter, I have outlined the theoretical and conceptual components inherent in investigating children's friendships 'at promise' in culturally diverse classrooms. The complex web of theoretical and conceptual underpinnings represented in this chapter all hinge on the potential of children's friendships as motivational contexts for learning in culturally diverse classrooms. Troyna and Hatcher (1992) represent many of the tensions in the research when they concomitantly contradict the 'contact hypothesis;' argue for a theory of relationships that includes harmony and conflict, notwithstanding developmental emphases; provide strong evidence on the existence of racism in children's everyday lives; but make clear the 'promise' of anti-racist attitudes even in the thinking of children who engage in racist behavior.

In Chapter 4, I will report on an ethnographic study which yielded the existence of two specific sociocultural themes in children's nonsynchronous 'promising' friendships in a fifth-grade culturally diverse classroom in a large urban elementary school in Atlanta, Georgia.

Chapter 3

Roots and Branches of Research on Children's Friendship in Culturally Diverse Classrooms

The research on children's friendships has developed along separate lines of investigation, despite the fact that these lines are bound together by common theoretical issues related to children's friendships in culturally diverse contexts. these lines of investigation are organized in this review under the following categories:

1. The etiology of scientific interest in children's friendships in the late nineteenth and early twentieth centuries;
2. Dominant developmental trajectories in children's conceptions of friendships;
3. Themes in mainstream sociological research on children's friendships, and;
4. Themes in research on children's friendships in culturally diverse classrooms; and selected recent studies that have attempted to problematize children's friendships 'at promise' in theoretically and conceptually fresh ways.

Etiology of Scientific Interest in Children's Friendships

The roots of sociological interest in children's friendships lie in the speculative theories of the late nineteenth and early twentieth century on the effects of social groups on human behavior (see Renshaw, 1981). Though the research climate of the early twentieth century was characterized by the absence of an empirical base for suppositions and ferment regarding conceptual issues such as the reality of social phenomena, group mind, and collective consciousness, pioneering sociologists and psychologists (for example, Cooley, 1902; Durkheim and Maus, 1966 [1903]; Mead, 1934; and Piaget, 1932) recognized that 'early social experiences — not merely with adults but with other youngsters — is centrally important to ontogenesis in many species' (Hartup, 1983, p. 104). Thematic continuities between Durkheim (Durkheim and Maus, 1966 [1903]), Mead (1934), and Bernstein (1960) indicate emphases on one's social circumstances as a determinant of one's cognitive processes. For example, Durkheim and Maus (1966 [1903]) believed that one's ability to classify objects was a result of one's experience of classifying people into social groups. Similarly, the social experiences typical of one's social class determined, for Bernstein (1960), the forms of language used and the way in which objects and people were classified.

Interestingly, when Piaget (1932) first advanced his theories of child development, the prospects augured well for concerted interdisciplinary studies of children's peer interactions (see Renshaw, 1981). Renshaw (1981) characterized the research climate of the period from the late 1920s to the beginning of World War II as:

> . . . a uniquely creative period in peer interaction research. The conditions that contributed to researchers' creativity included their openess to alternative paradigms and methodologies, the establishment of formal and informal networks . . . (p. 18)

By the late 1930s the prospects for a concerted thrust across disciplinary boundaries had dissipated with the emergence of Lewin and colleagues (1938, 1939) seminal work on the interdependence of children's behavior and context. Scholars interested in the social origins of peer interaction were given an impetus by Thrasher's (1927) pioneering work on peer and adolescent gangs in Chicago, an early example of symbolic interactionism in combination with participant observation. Thrasher's study represented 'the finest empirical research thereto published' (Renshaw, 1981, p. 2). His theoretical roots were grounded in the symbolic-interactionist tradition of Cooley's (1902) theory of social organization and Park's (1915) theory of ecological sociology. 'To demonstrate how an observer could study the mobile and unpredictable behavior of gangs in a natural setting' (Renshaw, 1981, p. 2), Thrasher developed new observational methods of participant observation.

Moreno's (1934) 'classic' sociometry for studying children's social choices, the *sociometric test*, was a method for studying children's social choices. According to Hartup (1983), 'no invention has had a greater impact on students of social psychology' (p. 106). Though Moreno (1934) is acknowledged as having made the most enduring contribution to the sociometric tradition, scholars such as Koch (1933) and Bott (1934) made significant contributions to this tradition during its fledgling period in the early 1930s. Bott (1934) used a diagrammatic representation to show group structure in his study of play activities in a preschool. Koch (1933) studied popularity among preschool children. He advanced a paired-comparison sociometric measure for determining individual differences between children who were having peer relations problems. His study showed that children's popularity correlated with behavioral indices of social adjustment such as ignoring others, playing alone, and aggression.

Scholars such as Jack (1934), Page (1936), and most notably, Lewin and Lippitt (1938), advanced experimental-interventionist studies of children's social relationships. Though experimental studies of children's social relationships can be traced to Triplett (1897), Lewin and Lippitt (1938) work on the social climate of children's groups provided the impetus for scholars to investigate why children behave as they do in different contexts.

Lewin and Lippitt (1938) argued for an approach to the study of group phenomena that retained a naturalistic setting while allowing the experimenter to intervene within 'a relatively free but well defined set of conditions' (p. 292). Lewin, Lippitt, and White (1939) conducted a study of autocratic, democratic, and *laissez-faire* styles of interaction between adults cast in various leadership roles and groups of boys. Their study showed that 'the interaction pattern of groups of boys was quite different under democratic and autocratic styles of leadership' (Renshaw, 1981, p. 15). Lewin, Lippitt, and White's study also pointed to the value of the field-experimentalist approach for identifying the determinants of social interaction. It was Lewin's approach to the study of group phenomena through an approach that combined a naturalistic setting with freedom for the experimenter to intervene within a 'relatively free but well defined set of conditions' (p. 292) that eventually dominated the developmental trajectory until the 1960s.

Developmental Thematic Trajectories

Numerous developmental psychologists have posited that the social origins of children's cognition lie in disequilibria (for example, Damon, 1983; Selman, 1980; Youniss, 1980). Specifically, developmental psychologists have searched for answers to questions concerning age differences in children's social understanding; if and when age differences are established, how are they characterized; the social and developmental processes through which children improve their understanding of social phenomena; the relations between developmental changes in children's social cognition and their everyday social conduct; and the role of affect in the development of social understanding (Damon, 1983).

Conceptions of Friendship

Findings on the relations between age and the nature of children's statements on social phenomena, notably friendships, represent a significant research line of inquiry on studies of ontogenesis from the preschool years through adolescence. Illustrations of Piagetian stage-like derivatives on children's friendship expectations include the works of Bigelow (1977), Selman (1980), and Youniss (1980). Hartup (1983) maintained that 'a number of studies reveal that both the conceptual system used by children to describe their friends, as well as specific expectations, undergo changes from the preschool years through adolescence' (p. 138).

Bigelow (1977) and Bigelow and LaGaipa (1975) coded essays written by

480 Canadian and 480 Scottish schoolchildren in the first through the eight grades on twenty-one dimensions of friendship expectations. Bigelow (1977) suggested that friendship expectations occur in the three loose stages:

1. a *reward-cost stage*, marked by the emergence of common activities, propinquity, and similar expectations, about the second or third grade
2. a *normative stage* in which sharing is evident — occurring at about the fourth or fifth grade, and
3. an *empathic stage* in which understanding, self disclosure, and shared interests emerge — about the fifth to seventh grade.

Berndt (1981) interviewed kindergarten, third-grade, and sixth-grade children using cartoons depicting friends or acquaintances. The study showed that children of all ages conceived friendship as involving shared activities, sharing of possessions, and absence of fighting. Youniss (1980) interviewed over 300 children ranging in age from 6 to 14 on definitions of friendship. The study highlighted the way children used notions about reciprocities in social relations. Between ages 9 and 11, understanding of reciprocity involved cooperation, interpersonal adjustments were conceived as mutual, and friends were believed to practice equality and equal treatment in their relations with each other. The possibilities inherent in Youniss's work for cross-disciplinary understanding of children's friendships will be discussed later in this chapter.

Selman (1980) studied the meaning and understanding of interpersonal relations in terms of general cognitive development. He tested the notion of a stage-like progression in the development of children's awareness of friendship. The program of research involved three phases:

1. initial interview methods to tap reflective thought
2. construct validation, and
3. application to other modes through which interpersonal understanding is expressed.

His study showed that parallels exist between children's awareness of friendship and general cognitive development. An applied variant of Selman's (1980) interview protocol for tapping children's reflective thought on their thinking will be discussed in greater detail in Chapter 4.

Disequilibria and Friendship

An illustration of disequilibria is evident in the disputes that friends have with nonfriends. Shantz (1987) has stated that 'conflict is an essential impetus to change, adaptation, and development' (p. 284). Friends tend to solve their disputes with minimal teacher intervention whereas teachers are often forced to intervene in disputes between nonfriends (Deegan, 1993; Rizzo, 1989).

Reputational bias provides another example of how children's friendships shift from what Selman (1980) described as preschoolers' focus on momentary playmates to what Hymel, Wagner and Butler (1990) described as elementary schoolchildren's focus on overall behaviors. For example, elementary school-children have differential perspectives on popular and unpopular children, often accepting certain behavior from popular children and rejecting the same behavior in unpopular children. Related research suggested that children's perspectives on aggressive dominance, often evident as an admirable quality, in preschool and kindergarten 'tough' children, compared to positive leader-ship in the early grades of the elementary school (see Pettit, Baski, Dodge, and Coie, 1990).

Mainstream Sociological Accounts

Interest in mainstream sociological studies of children's friendships is rooted in the early combined symbolic interactionist and participant observation studies of children's social relationships in the late 1920s. A typical feature of this research is an enduring focus on children's group processes. Two strands of research on group processes exist. One strand relies heavily on recent advances in sociometry. The other relies on the values of the symbolic-interactionist tradi-tion in research on group processes and focuses on friendship networks as 'sensitizing concepts' (Blumer, 1954, 1969, 1976). I will begin by briefly over-viewing the research findings of the sociometric tradition. Then I will follow with a more encompassing overview of a clutch of research studies that high-light the value of not only studying commonalties in children's friendship groups but also the value of exploring the diversity in the groups through investigations of individual perspectives in conjunction with intra- and inter-group perspectives.

Friendship Group Processes

Interest in group processes is rooted in the early studies of children's social relationships in the late 1920s (Renshaw, 1981). Hallinan (1980, 1981) identi-fied observational and sociometric approaches in the literature on children's friendship groups. The use of observational methodology to study friendship groups dates back to the late 1920s. Thrasher's (1927) study of 1,313 adoles-cent gangs in Chicago over a 7-year period showed that 'among the benefits of adolescent membership in a gang was a feeling of solidarity, high morale, group awareness, and attachment to local territory' (Hallinan, 1980, p. 324). Sherif, Harvey, White, Hood, and Sherif (1961) studied the effects of clique membership on the attitudes and behavior of 22 middle-class boys, all in the fifth grade. The study showed the emergence of two groups centering around task activities. Cliques were seen to form among individuals who must work interdependently to accomplish their goals. Hallinan (1980) identified five salient findings across clique studies:

1. members of friendship cliques are generally of the same sex, grade, and social class
2. informal ranking systems on the basis of status derive from the background characteristics and social behaviors of clique members
3. the clique exerts a pervasive influence over group attitudes and behaviors
4. membership in a clique has positive effects on self-image and self-confidence
5. adults generally fail to penetrate the friendship cliques of older youth. (pp. 325–6)

A second approach to the study of friendship cliques involves using sociometric data to detect cliques. Consistent findings in the literature show that only a small number of cross-sex friendships are made among elementary school-children (see Damico, 1974). In ethnically mixed schools, the large majority of friendship choices are to members of the children's own ethnic groups (Damico, 1974), and more exclusive friendships are likely to show a sex and ethnic cleavage. Other sociometric findings showed: that social class was associated with friendships, with children selecting the majority of their friends from their own social class (Langworthy, 1959); that sociometric status remained fairly stable over the period of an academic year (Lippitt and Gold, 1959); and that friendship choices tended to be associated with physical attractiveness (Dion and Berscheid, 1974), and academic achievement (Damico, 1974).

Cohen's (1977) study of the effects of pressures toward conformity, homophilic selection, and selective elimination of deviants or similarities among clique members stands out as the most comprehensive recent study of cliques based on sociometric data. Cohen (1977) defined a clique as four or more persons each of whom was involved in a mutual choice relation with at least two other persons in the subgroup. The study showed that initial homophilic selection accounted for homogeneity in groups over time and the broad range of uniformity found in groups.

In Britain, sociometric procedures have been heavily castigated as 'inferior' means of tapping the 'meaning of friendship for those involved' (see Denscombe, Szulc, Patrick, and Wood, 1986, p. 233). While I agree with Troyna and Hatcher (1992) that exclusive reliance on sociometry can potentially 'rigidify,' 'constrain,' and 'over-exaggerate' children's friendship nominations, I have also found that the creative use of picture-sociometric processes can frequently help establish rapport with children who are not comfortable with the highly verbal expectations and tenor of interview situations. This approach has particular potential with children who have minimal proficiency in the use of the English language. In Chapter 4, I will discuss a variant of a 'classic' picture-sociometric procedure that I found useful in a qualitative study of children's friendships in Atlanta, Georgia.

Children's Friendships in Culturally Diverse Classrooms

Friendship Lore and Language

In his writings on folklore as units of worldview, Dundes (1971) discussed 'lore' as present in all groups that share at least one trait. The Opies' (1959, 1969) studies of British children's street and playground language and lore are early examples of unexhausted sources of influence for children's friendship researchers. The Opies produced a rich compendium of the history and regional variations of British children's rhymes and games. Included in the Opies' studies were seasonal customs, initiation rites, superstitious practices and beliefs, rhymes and chants, catcalls and retorts, stock jokes, riddles, slang epithets, nicknames, and innumerable traditional games common in British schools. Salient in the Opies' view was the esoteric nature of children's culture. They wrote that children's culture 'is not for adult ears. It is at once more real, more immediately serviceable, and vastly more entertaining, than anything which they learn from grown-ups' (1959, p. 1). The Opies maintained that the protocols involved in children's friendships are ordered and rule governed. These protocols are characterized by a 'code of oral legislation.' The code includes such issues as making friends, making bargains, swapping, testing truthfulness, gaining possession of things, and keeping secrets.

Children's Perspectives and Friendships

Pollard (1985) studied the social structure and perspectives of 8–12-year-old children in a middle school located in a working-class community within a northern textile town in England. His study is useful in providing valuable perspectives on the combinative effects of race and gender. Pollard used a symbolic-interactionist theoretical framework in combination with ethnographic field methods. Although the school had a significant Asian intake, he focused his study on 80 11-year-old white children, who formed 58 per cent of the fourth year; there were 43 girls and 37 boys. He identified three basic cleavages in the children's social system based on age, sex, and race. Pollard identified three friendship groups: good groups, joker groups, and gang groups. He illustrated the differences among the three groups by considering their perspectives on various issues. Included in Pollard's discussion were the differences in inter-group attitudes under the following headings:

1. views of themselves and each other
2. outside the classroom
3. 'having a laugh' in class. (pp. 59–72)

The good groups valued the companionship and reliability of their 'small friendly groups' (p. 59). They distanced themselves from the more common activities of the other children, especially the gang groups. Segregation of boys and girls was a feature of the good groups. The boys and girls in the joker groups felt that the good groups were boring and 'didn't do anything' (p. 60). In contrast, they liked to be active and thought very little about gangs. The gang groups viewed the joker groups as 'show-offs' and 'bossy noses' (p. 61) and the good groups as 'no good,' 'teacher's pets,' 'goody-goodies,' and 'pathetic' (p. 61).

Outside the classroom, 'the good groups tended not to join in mainstream activities, and were in a marginal position within the children's social structure as a whole' (p. 62). In contrast, the joker groups were much more active, centered on playground activities, dinner-times, and 'meeting together outside school' (p. 63). Pollard noted that 'activities of this sort clearly bonded the group together' (p. 63). Games of chasing involved considerable degrees of excitement and flirtation, and were interesting 'when one realizes that in the classroom the girls regularly gave the impression of not mixing with the boys' (p. 65). Causing trouble and fighting characterized the activities of the gang groups outside of school. Fighting was the means to status within these groups. Fights involved preliminary rhetoric, such as 'pulping their nose,' 'smashing their teeth in,' and 'gobbing their nose' (p. 67); and unwritten codes demanded that a fair fight 'be between children of the same age and sex, and would generally be watched by others without interference and ignoring differences in size or strength' (p. 67).

The good group only broached 'having a laugh' if it was safe to do so. In contrast, the joker groups, as their name implied, were anxious to 'have a bit of fun' but, significantly, 'as a counter to boredom' and 'aware of the safety of laughing with or at the initiation of the teacher' (p. 69). The gang groups shared the joker groups' penchant for 'having a laugh' to counteract boredom, but differed to the extent that 'they were much more prepared to laugh at or despite the teacher' (p. 70).

An outcome of Pollard's (1985) work was his *model of coping strategies*. Although, he has recently combined this model with social-constructivist perspectives on processes of learning in context (see Pollard, 1994), the original model still represents one the more distilled versions of the interactionist tradition on children's social worlds in British primary schools. Four key aspects are:

1. an individual's ability to take active decisions based on their structural position;
2. an individual's 'interests-at-hand' in interaction processes based on their structural position;
3. the 'working consensus' negotiated in 'trade-off' between participants; and
4. strategic actions for coping with a particular setting based on conformity, negotiating, and rejecting. (1985, pp. 24–5)

Variants of these processes are resonant in many studies of children's friendships (see Corsaro and Eder, 1990; Davies, 1982; Deegan, 1993; Fine, 1987; Troyna and Hatcher, 1992).

Friendships and 'Idioculture'

Fine (1987) investigated preadolescent male cliques in the social world of Little League baseball. He conducted his study in five communities that reflected 'a range of middle class American communities' (p. 9), located in urban, suburban, and rural settings in the northeast and midwest. His theoretical perspective was symbolic-interactionist in the tradition of Cooley, Mead, Blumer, and Goffman. Data collection included participant observation, interviews, and questionnaires. Though he disclaimed the distinction of 'having compiled a complete ethnography of childhood' (p. 2), Fine suggested 'techniques by which all cultures could be analyzed — by seeing small groups connected to each other in networks of groups, producing through diffusion a *culture*' (p. 3).

Fine (1987) characterized preadolescent male clique friendships as involving a preoccupation with work-related activities, talk about sex, and opportunities for aggressive outlet. He emphasized the emergence of an idiosyncratic subculture peculiar to each group as a variant of a larger culture within society as a whole. According to Fine (1980), each friendship group develops its own culture, 'derived from past knowledge of members, norms of legitimate interaction, functional needs of the group, status and power considerations, and formulated by the particular events in which the group participates' (p. 316).

Variants on Nonsynchronous Children's Friendships in Culturally Diverse Classrooms

The literature on race, ethnicity, gender, and socioeconomic status developed as separate lines of inquiry. The early literature on race and schooling focused primarily on educational outcomes such as the comparison of black and white students' academic achievement in desegregated and non-desegregated schools; very little attention was given to social processes (see Grant, 1981).

In this section, I have attempted to avoid a reductionist or parallelist perspective on race, gender, and class features of cultural diversity in favor of a nonsynchronous approach. Accordingly, the focus here is on recent studies that have investigated race, gender, and class, or any combination of these on children's preadolescent social relationships in culturally diverse schools and classrooms. I begin by discussing two overarching strands in the literature on race and friendships. Then I address a variety of studies that address the nonsynchronous effects of race and friendships in combination with other sociocultural phenomena in classrooms and schools.

The 'Contact Hypothesis'

Troyna and Hatcher (1992) defined the *contact hypothesis* as 'the conviction that inter-personal contact across ethnic lines, in and of itself, brings about better race relations' (p. 24). Support for the contact hypothesis has become increasingly controversial (Aboud, 1988). Schofield (1981, 1982) argued that as a consequence of resegregation, proportions of each racial group in the school do not account for the whole story.

Recently, researchers have begun to examine other factors that might influence racial intergroup relations (see Hewstone and Brown, 1986). Aboud (1988) concluded that the results of research in the area of racial intergroup relations are probably the effects of exposure to rather than contact with another racial group. Troyna's and Hatcher's (1992) seminal work contradicts the 'contact hypothesis' that racial prejudice and discriminatory practices are dispelled by the positive experience of white and black children being together in school, and provides evidence 'that "race" is a significant feature of children's cultures in majority-white primary schools' (p. 195).

Short (1993) critiqued Troyna's and Hatcher's (1992) findings on ideological grounds. In contrast to their belief that the origins of prejudice derive from social and political structures, Short's (1993) approach is premised on the belief that prejudice is the product of ignorance. Despite the academic swordplay between proponents on both sides of this ideological divide, the rival camps are united in their belief that contact in and of itself does not improve children's race relations.

Children's Attitudes to Race

Lasker's (1929) classic study of adults' views of children's racial attitudes has had an undiminished influence in this area of research. His finding that children are 'made to notice outer differences and to accept them as signs of inner differences of value' (p. 329) has survived trenchant critiques of the methodology on children's racial attitudes. In their review of the research on children's attitudes to race, Carrington and Short (1992) flawed the 'classic' studies of Horowitz (1965), Clark and Clark (1947), and Davey (1983) for 'preventing fatuous task demands,' 'inflicting unnecessary pain,' and reinforcing prevailing stereotypes through 'forced choice' approaches (p. 200).

The assumption that children will automatically have 'racial' attitudes has also become a controversial issue. Miles (1988) coined the term *racialization* to caution against arbitrarily assuming that children will have racial attitudes. He used the concept of racialization to explain that race and race-related phenomena are context-specific. Miles (1988) maintained that it is futile to speak about children's racial attitudes if children have not experienced what it means to be directly or indirectly 'objectified' by appearances as a member of a given racial group. More recently, Gillborn (1995) has pointed out that racialized identities are not uniform phenomena, but nonsynchronous ones that are continually in flux:

> Race remains a vitally important part of contemporary life and politics, but it is neither separate from other factors (class, gender, sexuality,

disability) nor is it always the most important (essential) characteristic in human experience and action. Race may be more or less important to the same person at different times or in different contexts. This means, of course, that racism must be constantly and rigorously investigated, not simply asserted or denied according to some favored perspective. (p. 11)

In contrast to the long tradition of research on children's racial attitudes, little research exists that privileges children's voices on the role that race plays in their everyday lives and how these meanings become embedded in their own peer cultures. What is particularly lacking is research on the role that race plays in specific social 'settings' within specific institutional contexts — the family, the school, the community — and with distinctive cultures which embody social knowledge, attitudes, and values, and patterns of social relationships and strategies of interaction (see Troyna and Hatcher, 1992).

Social-race and Friendships

Clement, Eisenhart, and Harding (1979) were among the first researchers to examine social-race friendships. They investigated friendships as a central component in social-race relations in Grandin Elementary School, an urban desegregated school in North Carolina. The authors gathered ethnographic data in the course of a 2-year study in 1975–76. They focused on fifth- and sixth-grade students.

The authors avoided the use of the term *race* because they believed it implied a biological concept pertaining to populations. Instead, they used the term *social-race* or *color* because it implied a pseudobiological folk concept used primarily in reference to individuals. Aspects of social-race relations were discussed under the following headings: linguistic terms that people know and sometimes use; the interpretations that people sometimes give to their experiences; the norms that people attempt to encourage one another to follow, and the friendship patterns that tend to follow.

According to the authors, 'despite the divisive potential of social-race terminology and the interpretative framework of racism, and despite the relative lack of close friendship bonds, a degree of harmony was maintained' (1979, p. 54). The themes of 'informal segregation' and 'polite cooperation' emerged as significant factors in the harmony that was achieved at Grandin. The pattern of informal segregation was apparent in classes or during special activities where students chose their own seats; during free time when students congregated to play games; and at breakfast and lunch tables. The authors maintained that 'in spite of official concern over percentages of blacks and whites in classrooms and the subsequent effects on the formal system, evidence of separation of groups by social race was found at the informal level' (p. 54).

The authors claimed that 'polite cooperation' norms governed social-race relations at Grandin. These norms tended to suppress conflict on a short-term basis, at least. According to the authors,

> the disallowance of overt racism, the emphasis on politeness, and the emphasis on the teacher's duty as teacher and on the student's duty as student — regardless of the social-race identities of the individuals involved — could be seen as tending toward a situation in which conflicts were deemphasized and less likely to be given public expression. (pp. 54–5)

In sum, the limited harmony was achieved through the elimination of obvious patterns of discrimination. A significant finding of the study was that during the 2-year period, 'few close friendships developed' (p. 61), and social mechanisms rather than personal ties accounted for the harmony that was achieved (p. 61).

Race-gender and Friendships

Grant (1984) investigated the contribution of face-to-face interactions on the socialization of one race-gender group: black females in desegregated classrooms located in a working-class community in a large midwestern city. All classrooms represented first grades with 20 per cent or greater black student population. Ethnographic observations and interviewing methods were conducted in the classrooms of six female teachers; three white and three black. The author focused on four dimensions of classroom social life: teachers' evaluations of black females' skills; teachers' behaviors toward black females; black females' orientations toward teachers; and black females relationships with peers.

Grant discovered that teachers labelled white girls cognitively mature and 'ready for school,' whereas 'teachers did not see black girls as cognitively mature but rather as socially mature' (p. 102). Grant provided an interesting perspective on the Goffmanic concept of the *go-between*, 'a constituent member of two or more teams which have few positive ties' (p. 106). The author maintained that 'by playing the role of go-between black females likely made important contributions to the social integrations of desegregated classrooms' (p. 106). She characterized black females orientations toward teachers as ranging 'from apple-polishing to wary avoidance, with most falling in between' (p. 107). Specifically, black girls' contacts with their teachers were brief, task-related, and often on behalf of a peer rather than self.

Grant identified three major themes in her data on black females' relationships with peers: extent of contacts; helping relationships; and physical and verbal aggression. According to Grant, 'black girls had more extensive peer contacts than any other race-gender group' (p. 107), crossing race or gender lines more readily than any other children did in her study. Grant's study showed that black females 'gave peers academic aid and care' (p. 108). This care included comforting a child and helping to find a lost item. In return for their help, black females received nearly as much aid and care as they dispensed from diverse race-gender peers.

Grant discovered that most physical aggression was cross-gender. Black females differed from white females in their responses to threats. Unlike white girls 'who usually backed down, complied, or withdrew, or at most complained to the teacher' (p. 108), black girls 'fought back verbally or physically to more than half the aggression they encountered' (p. 108). Grant observed that black girls were the sole victims of the six racist remarks by white males recorded in five rooms. She pointed to the similarity in circumstance in each instance. Racist comments by white boys of low academic achievement invariably followed the teacher's commendation of a black girl's high academic achievement. Grant concluded that 'on the whole, however, black girls had more egalitarian relationships with peers than white girls' (p. 109). Grant's study was later used by McCarthy (1990) as an exemplar of the nonsynchronous dynamics of unequal social relations in a number of classrooms in the United States in his work on race identity and representation in education.

Cross-gender and Cross-race Friendships

Schofield (1981, 1982) investigated the complementary and conflicting social identities that developed between black and white children during the first three years of a middle school, referred to as 'Wexler.' This school was located in a large, industrial northeastern city. In addition, she analyzed the social processes that accounted for the development, maintenance, and change of these social relations. She was attracted to the research site because Wexler was designed 'to serve as a model of integrated schooling' (p. 9).

Schofield's study is particularly interesting because she set out to study a school that met or came close to meeting 'the conditions specified by Allport (1954) as conducive to development of intergroup attitudes and behavior' (p. 56). Schofield's primary data collection strategy was intensive and extensive observation in Wexler's classrooms, hallways, playgrounds, and cafeteria. A variety of other data collection strategies including interviews and sociometric questionnaires, were also used. Schofield used an eclectic data analysis strategy including sampling and triangulation techniques. Strategies to minimize observer reactivity and bias were used.

The study confirmed earlier findings regarding the rarity of cross-sex and cross-race early adolescent friendships, and that gender is a stronger grouping criterion than race, but she went beyond these findings to explain the meaning and explanations of the cleavages. She concluded that 'whereas relations with gender outgroups are profoundly influenced by the expectation of future ties, relations between blacks and whites are shaped by the history and present existence of racial separation, hostility, and discrimination in our society'

(p. 85). Under these circumstances, 'it is perhaps unrealistic to expect blacks and whites inside the school will form close and deep mutual relations easily or quickly' (p. 85).

Friendship Manoeuvres and Race Relations

Davies' (1984) study of 10- and 11-year-old children's social relationships in a large country town in northern New South Wales, Australia provides an interesting comparative perspective with British and American research. Her study included two Aboriginal girls, Sally and Teresa, and three Aboriginal boys, Henry, Warwick, and Roy. She conducted observations and conversations with children in classrooms and on the playground over a one-year period. Two central themes emerged from the study: (1) the paramount concern for children that friends 'be with you' and (2) that they 'should not pose' (p. 256).

Davies organized the children's statements into appropriate and inappropriate behaviors for a friend. Appropriate ways for friends to act included: plays nice, cooperates, helps do things for you, sticks by you, and shares. Inappropriate ways for friends to behave included: posing, not being cooperative, teasing, leaving you on your own, and being stupid. Davies (1984) argued that reciprocity was a critical construct embedded in ritualized behavior, having both positive and negative forms. The negative action of one child toward another makes it legitimate for the second child to pay it back. In her study she discovered that, in general:

> the children were aware of a differentness about Aboriginal adults and were aware of racial tension and prejudice between Aboriginal and white adults but they did not feel that this signified anything for their relationships with each other. (1984, p. 112)

Both the Opies (1959, 1969) mainstream accounts and Davies' (1982) ethnogenic account of Aboriginal children investigated the breaking of friendships. Although the Opies maintained that children 'make and break friends with a rapidity disconcerting to the adult spectator' (1959, p. 324), Davies (1984) advanced the view that this annoyance derives from the fact that the 'adult spectator does not actually understand what is going on' (p. 268). Davies (1984) also stated that children's 'friendships are in fact surprisingly stable. What appear to be breakages are, rather, manoeuvres within the friendship so that the functions friendship serves can be fulfilled' (p. 268). She identified the role of *contingency friends* as critical with respect to the functions that friendship serves. According to Davies, contingency friends are important in case it becomes necessary to leave a friend as a result of the friend's inappropriate behavior. 'Moreover, contingency friends increase the bargaining power of those children who know they will not be left alone if their friends chose to leave them in the event of a disagreement or fight' (1984, p. 261).

Interestingly, two of the Aboriginal boys, Henry and Roy, were noted for their capacity to fight and protect themselves from white prejudice, and also their willingness to serve as contingency friends. Davies (1982) summed up the perspectives of white boys on their Aboriginal classmates as follows:

> They fight to protect themselves, and generally, they don't fight these boys (unless, of course, 'it's called for'). As Ian says, 'Look you know Henry and Roy. We're Henry and Roy's friends and they don't bash us up at all' . . . Patrick says, 'One thing about Aboriginals, they, well, if you haven't got a friend, or anybody you can always turn to an Aboriginal person. (p. 112)

Friendships and Race, Gender, Class, Disability, and Community

Sleeter and Grant (1986) investigated 'the behavior, and the cultural knowledge of students, teachers, and administrators — especially that which focuses on the participants themselves as members of diverse social categories' (p. 10). These categories included racial groups, the sexes, and disability groups. The research site was a junior high school, referred to as 'Five Bridges,' located in a working-class neighborhood in a midwestern city. The 'rich diversity' (p. 10) in the student body attracted the authors to the school. School records reported 'the racial composition of 'Five Bridges' 580 students as follows: 0.5 per cent Asian, 2 per cent black, 28 per cent Hispanic, 2 per cent Native American, and 67.5 per cent white' (p. 10). The study used a combination of conflict-theoretical and anthropological perspectives to examine race, social class, sex, and disability features of cultural diversity and schooling and equality. The ethnographic case study design included: field observations, interviews, questionnaires, and document collection.

The authors discovered five kinds of students' friendships:

- best friends;
- friends one does things with;
- friends one does some things with;
- girl/boyfriends; and
- non-romantic girl/boyfriends.

The first three kinds of friendships were with members of the same sex. Sleeter and Grant maintained that 'distinctions among these three kinds of friends depended on two factors: the level of trust and intimacy between two individuals, and the number of things one did or the amount of time one spent with that individual' (p. 27). The remaining two types of friendships were cross-sex friendships: girl/boyfriend; and non-romantic friends. 'Non-romantic friends typically included members of the opposite sex that the student had known for a long time and talked to in school, but did not date' (p. 27). The authors reported that 'several students did not name any friends in one or two of the categories' (p. 27). Interestingly, 'several students said that they were not yet interested in the opposite sex, so all their friendships were with members of the same sex' (p. 27).

According to Sleeter and Grant, 'Five Bridges students believed that one could achieve any kind of social image and reputation by controlling one's own behavior, and no one should be excluded from status, popularity, or friendship on the basis of ascribed characteristics such as race, sex, social class, or handicap' (p. 62). The authors explained the determinants of students' knowledge about human diversity in terms of the following community and school factors: (1) 'Students' interracial friendships were influenced by the racial makeup and distribution of the community, the community's value for getting along, residents' common lifestyle, and geography' (p. 186). (2) 'Students' cultural knowledge about gender was influenced by the local economy, the community lifestyle, community values defining family responsibilities, the media and school-related factors' (p. 195). (3) 'Students' cultural knowledge about social class was influenced by parents' work roles, family income levels, and school factors' (p. 198).

Two Bridging Studies of Children's Friendships

Although Vygotskian theories essentially focused on the social origins of individual development, they gave impetus to what are often grouped as interpretive theories of the social origins of cognition. Interpretive theories have attracted the interest of scholars from diverse disciplinary traditions (Bruner, 1986; Corsaro, 1985; Corsaro and Eder, 1990; Corsaro and Rizzo, 1988). Corsaro and Eder (1990) claimed that interpretive scholars are united in their belief that children's cognition is a 'collective process that occurs in a public rather than a private realm . . . stressing that children discover a world endowed with meaning and help to shape and share in their own developmental experiences through their participation in everyday cultural routines' (p. 199). Interestingly, the interpretive model does not reject stage-like theories but recasts them within a productive-reproductive process of 'increasing density and reorganization of knowledge that changes with children's developing cognitive and language abilities and with changes in their social worlds' (p. 200).

Much of the impetus for interpretive theories in education has been generated by Giddens' (1984) sociological theory of structuration (see Chapter 2). One significant outcome of this challenge has been the emergence of fresh perspectives on the themes of access to cultural resources and differential adult treatment that have traditionally been central to cultural reproduction theories of education. Interpretive researchers have branched out into children's worlds of playmates in playgroups and nursery schools.

Corsaro's Study of an Italian Scuola Materna

Corsaro and Eder (1990) have begun to elaborate a derivative of Giddens' work described as *interpretive reproduction* (p. 200). They describe the core of interpretive reproduction as not merely what Vygotskian theorists might describe as 'internalization' of the adult world, but a process whereby 'children become part of adult culture through their negotiations with adults and their creative production of a series of peer cultures with other children' (p. 201).

Constructing a hybrid theoretical framework derived from Bruner's (1986) psychology of mind and Gidden's sociological theory of duality in structure and agency, Corsaro and Rizzo (1988) examined a process whereby children not only made knowledge their own but did so in the community of a pre-school — 'scuola materna' in Bologna, Italy. These researchers used a three-layered analysis of the routine of 'discussione' — 'what Italians refer to as . . . a verbal routine of the culture that children engage in with adults and peers from a very early age' (p. 882) — to examine the socialization processes in the scuola materna. The central finding that emerged from this study was that children's collective creative productions of peer culture are influenced by and contribute to the reproduction of the adult world. Specifically, their work highlights how children's shared knowledge and activities were affected by the change from their scuola materna to the elementary school and the concomitant exposure to adult information on age grading which affected their appropriation of the adult world and provided insights on their own peer cultures.

In terms of thematic trajectories, Corsaro's studies (see Corsaro, 1994) clearly indicate an extension of constructivist theories on how children make social knowledge by acting on their environments. The integrative functions of nursery schoolchildren's friendships include gaining access, building solidarity and mutual trust in, and protecting the interactive space of playgroups. The combining of constructivist and interactionist theories and methods will be revisited when I examine the possibilities for interdisciplinary research on children's friendships in Chapter 8.

Troyna and Hatcher's Study of Race and Egalitarianism in Children's Friendships

Troyna and Hatcher (1992) examined 10- and 11-year-old children's social relationships against the backcloth of 'race' and 'racism' in two neighboring local education authority schools in England which were described as 'Greenshire' and 'Woodshire.' They attempted to explain how children reproduce racism as a popular ideology in daily life, and how they articulate their meanings and understandings of racism with their existing social relationships. In their study, Troyna and Hatcher (1992) found that the interplay of processes of domination and equality were closely related to race and racism in children's cultures in predominantly white primary schools. They identified racist

name-calling as an important strategy 'within many children's interaction reper-
toires (though not in "others") . . . in the context of children's cultures, relationships, and processes of social interaction' (pp. 196–7). Troyna and Hatcher
(1992) maintained that the connections between children's intricate web of
social relationships and racism often operates in 'complex, sometimes contradictory ways with other elements of children's commonsense understanding of
their lives' (p. 196).

In a recent elaboration of the pedagogical consequences of their ongoing
work on the reproduction of race as a popular ideology, Troyna and Hatcher
(1992) provided an interesting developmental complement to their previously
argued critical theories of race and racism derived from Gramsci's (1977) concept of 'hegemony.' Using Youniss's (1980) research on the changes that take
place as children move into and through the period of middle childhood,
Troyna and Hatcher (1992) found much common ground with Youniss's
emphases on the themes of equality and reciprocity in children's peer cultures.
Youniss's (1980) research was also discussed as an exemplar of recent derivatives
of Piagetian stage-like theories earlier in this chapter.

While Troyna and Hatcher (1992) argue that the Piagetian legacy needs to
be rendered 'more social,' the authors make the significant point that psychological studies are potent references for sociological studies of children's peer
relationships. This is a far cry from the critiques of Harré (1986), for example,
who castigated developmental perspectives for their adherence to individualism,
abstract conceptions of friendships, and the endpoints of development to a
more integrative cross-disciplinary working position. Specifically, Troyna and
Hatcher (1992) capture the potency of these contradictory 'tensions' with reference to variations on the theme of equality in children's peer relationships:

> Children do not necessarily confront each other as equals. On the
> contrary, they live in a social field structured by ideologies of gender,
> class, 'race,' age, ability, and so on, which tend to position children
> unequally in relation to each other. Other ideologies speak to them of
> equality, and as we have argued, drawing on Piaget's insight, the most
> powerful among them is that deriving from, and continuously rein-
> forced by, everyday peer interaction. (p. 123)

Conclusion

The studies reviewed in this chapter provide a complex picture of children's
friendships in culturally diverse classrooms. They provide insights on stereotypical patterns in children's friendships based on inclusion and exclusion, and
suggest that we need to go beyond reciprocal, parallelist, and symmetrical frameworks if we are to understand what it is like to be and have friends in today's
increasingly diverse classrooms. They also suggest that children's friendships

are influenced in nonsynchronous or contradictory ways by the interactive outcomes of race, ethnicity, gender, class, and community, and other life-situational sociocultural factors in children's social lives. One critical finding that augurs well for future studies is the growing consensus in diverse research traditions that children's friendships show 'promise' as motivational contexts for learning in the present culture of public school classrooms.

Chapter 4

Children's Friendships in a Fifth-grade Culturally Diverse Classroom in Atlanta, Georgia

In this chapter, I draw attention to the potentially harmful effects of evaluating children's friendships on what are often negative outcomes, rather than on the efforts that children make to effectively negotiate their friendships. In the study reported here, children's friendships in a fifth-grade culturally diverse class in a large urban elementary school in Atlanta, Georgia, in the southeastern United States, indicated the existence of nonsynchronous patterns.

Two interrelated sociocultural findings emerged in the study. First, the children who negotiated their friendships within their own tacitly agreed upon parameters experienced consonance in their relationships. Second, the children who negotiated their friendships beyond their own tacitly agreed upon parameters experienced contextual dissonance in their relationships. In the cases of the children with contextually dissonant friendships the influence of life-situational challenges related to drugs, transiency, and being a runaway became salient.

This study examined what it is like to be and have friends and how developing conceptions of friendship become embedded in children's peer culture. In complement and counterpoint to conventional views which stress intrapersonal factors such as social skill deficits, the focus in this study was on external or life-situational influences on children's friendships. For this study, it was necessary to choose a definition of children's friendships that could potentially lead to evidence on children's reflective thoughts on the influence of their life-situational experiences on their own friendships. Fine's (1981) threefold-interactionist definition which operationalizes friendship as 'a staging area for interaction, a cultural institution for the transmission of knowledge and performance techniques, and a crucible for the shaping of selves' (p. 41) was chosen for this study (see Chapter 1). The findings reported here are culled from a larger study that investigated more broadly the dynamic of children's friendships in the same fifth-grade class (see Deegan, 1990).

Participants, Context, and Data Collection Procedures

Ethnographic observations took place in a 'bellwether' (Goetz and LeCompte, 1984) or highly developed instance of cultural diversity in one fifth-grade classroom, '5C,' in a large urban elementary school. The sample included twenty-four children, 46 per cent were male and 54 per cent were female. Racial/ethnic distribution was as follows: Anglo 13 per cent, African-American 54 per cent, Asian 16 per cent, and Hispanic 17 per cent. The Asian children were from Cambodia, China, Iran, and Iraq. Three of the Hispanic children were from Mexico and one was from Columbia. The majority of participants lived in nearby housing projects with a dwelling-type distribution as follows: single family 27 per cent, duplex 20 per cent, and apartment 53 per cent. There were approximately 67 per cent of the students on free or reduced-price lunch programs. The teacher, Ms. Oldham, had twenty years' teaching experience.

Observations

Observations took place during half-day observation periods (alternating between morning periods defined as 8:00 am to 12:00 am, and afternoons defined as 12:00 am to 3:00 pm), twice-weekly on varied days of the week, between August and March. These observations covered normal classroom activities and noninstructional periods such as transitions, lunchtime, and recess. Systematic efforts were made to fully engage in experiencing the setting while simultaneously trying to make sense of it all (see Chapter 5). Because so few studies had investigated children's friendships in culturally diverse schools, Glaser and Strauss's (1967) constant comparison method guided data collection and analysis.

Interviews

Informal interviews and interview guide approaches were used (Patton, 1980). Informal interviews were conducted throughout the study. They varied from momentary exchanges to brief conversational interludes, often occurring during transition times. Successive rounds of interviews, which usually extended 10, 15, or 20 minutes, were conducted in October, January, and March. Interview topics were derived from focus topics grounded in the emerging theory (for example, fights, children with friendship-making difficulties, new friends, contingent friends). Strategies for enhancing a nonthreatening interview situation included joking about the size of the microcassette recorder, playing tapes at various speeds, and a guarantee that interviewees would have an opportunity to listen to and respond to the views that they had expressed during their interviews. All interviews took place in a library storeroom with both interviewer and interviewee at the participant's level at a small circular table. All interviews were audio recorded using a voice-activated microcassette recorder, and later transcribed.

The majority of the children had poor verbal skills and difficulty in articulating their feelings on such a complex interpersonal construct as friendship. In this regard Selman's (1980) study of the parallels that exist between children's awareness of friendship and their general cognitive development proved useful. Using a modified version of Selman's (1980) approach, interviews included three phases:

1. Initial interviews to tap the children's reflective thoughts on their friendships.
2. Further interviews to dimensionalize or 'tease out' emergent features of friendships.
3. Final interviews to examine how children negotiated the parameters of their friendships.

The children's interview data were characterized by terse responses and difficulty in providing applied examples of the expressive dimensions of their friendships. As a consequence, the majority of data sources were one- and two-word utterances, clausal statements, and single sentences; only a few examples of sentence clusters were recorded.

Sociograms

A modified version of Hallinan's (1981) roster technique was used in conjunction with McCandless and Marshall's (1957) picture-sociometric technique. This hybrid technique has proven to yield reliable and valid data with preschoolers with limited reading skills (see Pellegrini, 1987). The technique was adopted for the following reasons:

1. The poor reading skills of the children, generally.
2. The enrollment flux with the attendant difficulty for children to keep abreast of newly arrived children's names, especially those of immigrant children.
3. The language difficulties of immigrant children in understanding verbal protocols.

Color 3-inch by 5-inch children's photographs were randomly ordered in rows of 6-across and 4-down on a 3-foot square, white mat-cardboard. Children's names were printed underneath the photographs with black feltpen. Children were asked to respond on a questionnaire to other children in their class in terms of 'Best Friend,' 'Friend,' and 'Don't Know.' Tests were administered following the first two rounds of individual interviews with the children in October and January. Sociograms were constructed to assist with conceptual clarity. An example of a sociogram that was constructed during the study is illustrated in Figure 4.1.

Physical-trace Documents

According to Goetz and LeCompte (1984), physical trace collection methods involve the location, identification, analysis, and evaluation of 'the erosion and

Figure 4.1:   Sociogram based on best friend choices for Test 1

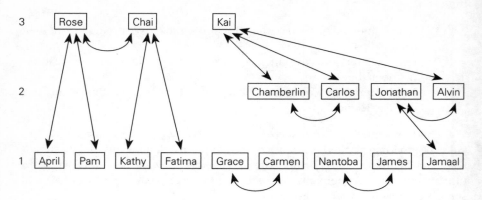

Note: Lena and Martha were absent. Keshia, Taylor, and Donna did not reciprocate choices. Keshia asked to reciprocate with Latoya, a nonpermission student, who was listed. Taylor and Donna did not reciprocate on the test, or request to reciprocate with nonlisted students.

accretion of nonsymbolic and natural objects used by people' (p. 154). Children's message notes, self-memos, and doodling are examples of the artifacts that were collected. Also collected were artifacts such as calendars, school rules and regulations, and weekly enrollment and demographic reports.

Analysis

Throughout the eight-month data collection period, I constantly analyzed the observation, interview, sociometric, and physical trace data from the accumulated data bank. I incorporated three forms of triangulation to establish confidence in the interpretation of the data:

1. Interview, observation, sociograms, and documents were compared.
2. Data from individual children were compared with data from other children.
3. Data collected from children were compared with data from adult participants.

Collection of data involved searching for key and recurrent events and activities that became categories of focus for further observation and interviewing (for example, early categories included making friends, expressing friendship, gender demarcation). Instances of the categories were collected to determine the diversity of dimensions under the category (for example, the recurring incident of togetherness was expanded to include sharing). The data was continually analyzed for an emerging model to discover basic social processes. In addition, discrepant examples were analyzed to consider their relevance to the categories and relationships that emerged.

Reflexivity

Ethical obligations regarding researcher role and bias were identified and tracked. As a result of the fact that 'data must go through the researcher's mind before it is put down on paper' (Bogdan and Biklen, 1982, p. 42), I was concerned with the effect that my own subjectivity might have on the data that I was collecting in the study. Erickson (1984) described the challenge as not so much a matter of objectivity but one of 'disciplined subjectivity' (p. 61). In line with Strauss's (1987) advise to 'mine your experience, there's gold there' (p. 11) and Peshkin's (1988) exhortation to 'tame subjectivity' (p. 20), I attempted to limit biases, while remaining cognizant of the fact that I could not eliminate them.

In my relationships with the children I actively cultivated the role of 'friendly cultural stranger' because it allows for flexibility and considerable research bargaining with early adolescent children. Accordingly, moralistic judgments were kept to a minimum, especially in cases of racist and sexual talk. Mindful, as Hammersley (1983) pointed out, that reflexivity includes the 'recognition that research is a social activity' (p. 3), I kept a reflexive account of the biases that I experienced during the course of the study and the strategies that I used to deal with what Goetz and LeCompte (1984) referred to as 'the personal predilections that are unavoidable at times' (p. 238). In Chapter 5 I provide a reflexive account of the approach that I used to keep track of my roles and relationships in this study.

LeCompte's (1987) guidelines for identifying bias and subjectivity helped me track biases with reference to personal and professional themes. Specifically, my schooldays and teaching experiences took place in all male Roman Catholic institutions in sharp contrast to the particular cultural context where my study took place. My understanding of life in the United States was a vicarious one, essentially derived from popular media images of racial and ethnic dissonance. These biases were tracked in theoretical memos, observer comments on the margins of field notes, and in a research log for this purpose (Bogdan and Biklen, 1982). The intention was to limit biases, remaining cognizant of the fact that they could never be eliminated. I arranged both formal and informal opportunities to discuss these biases with research colleagues, school administrators, and the classroom teacher.

Children's Negotiation of Friendships within Their Own Tacitly Agreed Upon Parameters

Two major themes emerged in this investigation. The first theme is *consonance* — the negotiation of children's friendships within the children's tacitly agreed upon parameters. The majority of children exhibited characteristics or traits that were valued by the class as a whole. Consonant negotiation of friendships involved strategic adaptation to the parameters of *encounter, togetherness, niceness, and fighting* in the children's everyday routines, rituals, and activities.

Encounter

The parameter of encounter was critical for the promotion of friendships with new students. Although the teacher was instrumental in promoting encounters within the classroom (see Deegan, 1990), the focus here is on children's negotiated encounters. These encounters frequently took place when the students had the opportunity to negotiate freely and openly without teacher interference; usually this happened on the playground at recess.

Children's negotiated encounters were simple low verbal protocols. The flux in class enrollment ensured frequent rehearsals of these ritualistic protocols. Features of the ritual were: the approach, the exchange of names, cursory small-talk, and the invitation to play. The children highlighted the salience of 'going up to them' (the new students), exchanging names, and the inconsequential nature of the rest of the interaction. Although not all children explained 'encounter' as an invariant sequence, the majority spoke about the symbolic approach of 'going up to them.' Jonathan, an African-American male explained: 'Just ask them what's their name and stuff, and get to know them.' Alvin, an African-American male who shared a best friend relationship with Kai, a Cambodian male, explained: 'They just tell them their names . . . and if they like you . . . they'll be your friend.' Although a group of students rather than two or three made the approach, the ritual of 'going up to them' usually left the initiate with a friend or friends.

In the present study, children's moves toward friendship were generally similar to what Rizzo (1989) has described as 'unilateral' friendship displays in his study of first-grade children in a small town in the midwestern United States. The children attempted to overcome cultural barriers in their situations through friendship bids. This finding is consistent with the studies of Opie and Opie (1959, 1969) and Davies (1984) who argued that reciprocity was embedded in children's ritualized behavior, but contrasts with their finding that children's initial encounters were promoted by highly verbal protocols.

Togetherness

The parameter of togetherness implied being present for a same-sex friend. Evidence indicated that it cut across racial, ethnic, and socioeconomic factors in the social lives of the children. James, an African-American male, explained: 'They just sit there and talk awhile.' As indicated in James's comment, sharing was an important dimension in togetherness. Children included sharing conversation (for example, 'talk about boys,' 'talk about different teachers'); play (for example, 'swim,' 'jump-rope,' 'skipping,' 'go places together'); and work (for example, 'work together,' 'help each other') in their discussions of togetherness. Nantoba, an African-American male, elaborated the significance of talk in friendships: 'Like, at home, you can really express your feelings with a friend. At school you barely have time to talk. Like, today, doin' reading, you can't talk in class. Lunchroom we can't talk. We have to whisper.'

Togetherness also manifested itself in the sharing of a single dimension, but could involve an interactive dimension such as sharing material things for play (for example, checkers and Nintendo). The children's perspectives indicated that being available to share was generally more important than whatever activity, routine, or interaction took place later. Several children referred to the importance of 'borrowin',' 'buyin',' and 'givin' stuff' to their friends.

Niceness

The parameter of niceness was equated with sharing and respect among children, and these concepts were threads in the diffusive theme of reciprocity in the children's social relationships. Being nice emerged repeatedly as a response to the perennial question: What is a friend? Niceness was conceptualized in terms of expressive dimensions. Chai, a Chinese female, explained: 'I guess try and be nice to them and respect them.' In response to the question 'What is being nice?' Rose, an Anglo female, replied: 'Nice is that you give your friend somethin'. You give it right back to her. You share things.' Rose's comments were typical of those of several other children of varying race, ethnicity, and socioeconomic status, who subsumed the concept of sharing within their view of being nice.

Another example of sharing and niceness was evidenced in the way that the Mexican children and the Columbian female in the class negotiated the nuances and subtleties of Mexican and Columbian-Spanish dialects with each other. This group noted differences but attributed these to country-of-origin, rather than to ethnic inferiority. The Spanish-speaking females generally revealed playful respect for these differences rather than any class value-laden references.

Fighting

The parameter of fighting emerged as a manoeuvre in the way that several children negotiated their friendships. Although fights became part of the children's lore, the after-effects of fights were short-lived affairs. James explained: 'After two days, they be friends again.' Similarly, Rose, an Anglo female, explained the short-lived after-effects of her fight with Donna, an African-American female: 'Then the next day, she started to be nice to me. Then I got to know her, and then we got to be friends.' Carlos, a Mexican male, was unequivocal on the after-effects of fights: 'It doesn't matter, they're still friends.'

Fights between friends occurred infrequently, and the children's popular perception of fighting was that only nonfriends fought. Donna, an African-American female who was involved in some of the most public fights in the class, explained that 'friends hardly ever fight.' In contrast to many of the teachers who viewed fighting as deviant, however, some children's interview transcriptions, such as those of James, Carlos, and Rose, indicated that they viewed fights as having a salutary effect on their friendships.

Some children described the defense of a friend as a legitimate cause for a fight. In such instances the time-honored tradition of standing up for your friends emerged. Lena, an African-American female, described her fight with Donna as follows: 'There was this girl named Keshia. They were foolin' each other. You know hittin' each other, like. She tried to kick Keshia under the table and she kicked me. And I said quit kickin' me. She said, "So, I don't have to." She roll up her eyes and we have a fight.' Similarly, Alvin, an African-American male, explained how third parties can intrude on friends when they are playing and cause a fight: 'Yea, like I be playing basketball with my friend. I be a captain. Other boys come to my friend and say, "he not your captain" and pick a fight.'

Findings in the present study overlap with those of Opie and Opie (1959) and Davies (1984) who investigated the breaking of friendships. Opie and Opie maintained that 'children make and break friendships with a rapidity disconcerting to the adult spectator' (p. 324). In the present study several adult spectators expressed their concerns about the physically injurious effects of fighting. Whereas the teachers were interested in a policy of containment, the children were interested in the negotiating strategies of fighting. On this point, Davies advanced the view that 'children's friendships are in fact surprisingly stable. What appears to be breakages, are, rather, manoeuvers within the friendship so that the functions friendships serve can be fulfilled' (p. 268).

Children's Negotiation of Friendships at the Extremes and Beyond Their Own Tacitly Agreed Upon Parameters

The second theme that emerged in the present study is *dissonance* — the negotiation of children's friendships at the extremes and beyond the children's tacitly agreed upon parameters. Rosenberg (1975) defined as *contextual dissonance* being a member of a minority not valued by the majority in the classroom. Rosenberg stressed that the negative consequences of minority status within the immediate context derive from the fact that social comparison processes operate more forcefully at the face-to-face level rather than when society at large is the frame of reference (see Chapter 3). *Immigrant dissonance* and *life-situational dissonance* are social categories of dissonance that emerged in the present study.

Immigrant Dissonance

Immigrant children experienced popular misconceptions about their culture. Evidence of dissonance included derogatory comments on the status of their health, difficulties with language, and physical appearance, and name-calling. On popular fears about immigrants as carriers of disease, Rose, an Anglo female, stated: 'Sometimes they don't want that person to get near them, cause they speak like they have rabies, or somethin.' James, an African-American male, also referred to the fears of disease, and stated: 'They test them for diseases before they bring them over.' There was general agreement among both immigrant and nonimmigrant children that children from other countries experienced difficulty in making friends. Language was the most frequently observed and cited difficulty. Keshia, an African-American female, explained: 'It's hard for them to get a friend without speakin' their language.'

Although language difficulties were readily acknowledged, both immigrant and nonimmigrant children were slow to admit that children from other countries were often the butt of name-calling and insults. Derogatory names that were overheard or described in interview transcriptions included: 'Jalapeno,' 'Cambodian fool,' 'Jungle people,' 'Chink,' and 'Spaniola.' 'Jalapeno' was the only racist comment that I heard. All other examples of racist innuendo derived from interview probes to children to tell the author about the names that students use to give children from other countries a hard time. The single most penetrating abuse was directed toward Kai, a Cambodian male. Although interview evidence indicated that Kai had many friends in the class, he was not an exception from racist comments. Alvin, his African-American friend indicated that Kai's physical appearance had proven the butt of racist comments: 'They don't like his face shape and stuff.'

Racial and ethnic misclassifications leading to name-calling and in one instance a serious fight were evidenced. Jonathan, an African-American male who had earlier indicated his intolerance of Spanish-speaking students by saying: ''Cause they be talkin' how they bring brothers to America, or somethin' like that . . . like Spanish people' went on to misclassify Anusch, a newly arrived Iranian boy, as: 'This Spanish boy Anusch, he's nice, but he be talkin' too much.' This led to a violent attack by Jonathan on Anusch. In a group interview in March, Jonathan, Alvin, Chamberlin, and Jamaal, all African-American males became side-tracked in a discussion as to whether Anusch, the newly arrived Iranian male, could speak Spanish and who had heard him doing so. The boys reached the consensus that he was Mexican and could speak Spanish.

Immigrant children also wrestled with acculturation, assimilation, and accommodation concerns and issues. In an interview with Carmen, who acted as a 'go-between' for Spanish-speaking children, the compounding difficulties of being ethnically misclassified and her personal dilemmas with assimilation and accommodation tensions emerged: 'Some people think I am from Mexico, because of the way I talk. I talk like I don't know a lot of English.' She expressed this frustration after being assigned to help Martha, a newly-arrived

Columbian female. Although these girls liked to play with language and lots of giggling took place when Carmen helped Martha, Carmen stated that Martha's Columbian Spanish was 'hard to understand'. In the same breath she explained her struggles with ethnic identity and stated that she was 'mostly Mexican, but living in America'. Much of Carmen's struggle related to the fact that having lived in the United States for most of her life, she was at a different benchmark on the acculturation–assimilation continuum than more newly arrived Hispanic children. At the same time she had to contend with the popular class misconception that she was Spanish-speaking and therefore not American.

Life-situational Dissonance

Although several children exhibited traits or characteristics not valued by the majority of children in the study, the experiences of Jonathan, Lena, and Donna, were the most intense. At the root of the problem was a disjunction between their school and home social worlds. These children's friendships provided evidence of unique 'mixes' of contingencies (McCarthy, 1990) that affected their individual friendship negotiating strategies.

Jonathan

Jonathan, a 12-year-old African-American male, was the most affected by the disjunction between his home and school situations as evidenced by his struggles to negotiate his friendships within the children's tacitly agreed upon parameters of friendship. He lived with his mother — a single parent and crack-cocaine addict — his teenage sister, and her infant child. Jonathan often responded to situations in ways that made his friends wary of him. As Carlos, a Mexican male, stated: 'Jonathan would be in a gang.' Nantoba, an African-American male who protected Jonathan from himself during violent outbursts, stated that he often had 'to hold Jonathan back'. Jonathan's theft of a bicycle, unexplained facial cuts and bruises, and chronic absenteeism led to 'catch up' with his schoolwork, and reassigned seating. In a classroom where togetherness, niceness, sharing, and knowing how far you could go with fighting were highly valued parameters of friendship, Jonathan had serious difficulties.

Lena

Lena, a 13-year-old African-American female, was the oldest participant in the study. She was physically more mature than her classmates. Lena lived with her single-parent mother, but occasionally stayed with her sister in another part of the city during times of domestic stress. The precariousness of her situation was revealed in the dramatic change of her friendship ratings from the first to the second round of interviews. Although nominated in interviews as one of the most popular children in the class her stature decreased to one of the least popular. Lena showed a pattern of ever increasing absence from school. During her absences rumors were rife that she was pregnant and unable to return to school. Nantoba, an African-American male, stated: 'Everyone say she's overweighted and she's pregnant.' Given the stress that third party influences exerted on friendships, this gossip helped push the parameters of Lena's best friendship with Frances, another African-American female, to a breakdown. Lena fuelled gossip with her frequent stories and denials of purported pregnancies in her housing project. In March, Lena's mother filed a missing persons report. At the conclusion of the study she had been missing from school for four weeks.

Lena's friendships were affected by her absences from school. To her credit, her classmates viewed her as having positive qualities as evidenced by their initial view of her as a popular child. Like Jonathan, however, she was not often with them. Days and weeks passed by and distance between Lena and her friends became critical. As the subject of ridicule, she lost friends in a class where being together was critical and being ridiculed was sufficient to breach the parameters of children's friendships.

Donna

Donna, an African-American female, was described by the teacher as 'her own worst enemy.' She was the daughter of transients who lived in a nearby motel. Donna arrived in class in late October. She was not receptive to new friends and resisted the routine friendship bids of her classmates: 'If they wouldn't make friends with me, I wouldn't make friends with them.' She preferred to try and establish status through athletic and gymnastic displays on the playground. She sat in a single desk behind the radiator which had been placed there out of the way rather than as an appropriate seating location. In every socially promising situation her response was negative. In reference to a fight that she had experienced she stated: 'Sometimes they accuse me of doin' somethin' and I don't do it.' She was the only student who qualified her response on the healing that follows fights by stating that only 'sometimes people come together after fights.' On her relationships with immigrant children, she was equally hostile. She stated: 'I don't really know what they think, or anythin.' 'Cause they hardly ever hang around me.'

In late January Donna left Stanley Hazel Elementary School. In a classroom where the majority of children actively promoted friendships in ritualistic protocols, Donna was the antithesis of what friendship was all about. In an ironic twist on the student's view of the parameter of togetherness in the negotiation of their friendships, Donna's response was perhaps due in part to her efforts to insulate herself from the prevailing socially promising environment in order to deal with the next change of address in her life.

Jonathan, Lena, and Donna did not effectively negotiate the parameters of their friendships. They experienced special impediments in doing so. Unlike other children who routinely stretched the parameters of their friendships, these children subverted the tacitly agreed upon parameters of friendships and social relationships through what their classmates perceived as maladaptive responses. Their individual responses were influenced by significant life-situational dissonances in their home social worlds which carried over into the social context of their fifth-grade classroom. I will revisit Jonathan's, Lena's, and Donna's stories, and relate them to Pollard's (1990) stories of Daniel and Sally when I discuss friendships as motivational contexts for social learning in Chapter 8.

Challenges of Friendships 'At Promise'

This study affirms the centrality of children's friendships in the social world of early adolescent children in culturally diverse elementary schools. Two major interrelated sociocultural themes emerge in these findings. The analysis indic- ates that the two heuristically separate themes are in fact interrelated and socioculturally bound. One theme is that children's friendships are potentially *consonant* — what I have argued is the negotiation of children's friendships within tacitly agreed upon parameters. Consonant negotiations of friendships took place within the parameters of encounter, togetherness, niceness, and fighting. Gender proved the strongest grouping criterion for friendships, but children also exhibited friendships across racial, ethnic, and socioeconomic linking patterns. Several of the children's friendships involved linking patterns across racial groupings that included the majority African-American student group with Asian, Hispanic, and Anglo children.

The second theme is that children's friendships are potentially *dissonant* — what I have argued is the negotiation of children's friendships at the extremes and beyond the children's tacitly agreed upon parameters. Although there was evidence of some racial and ethnic dissonance, life-situational dissonance emerged as a more significant problem. Some children experienced contingent mixes of life-situational factors related to drugs, transiency, and being a runa- way in their friendships. These children's friendship negotiating attempts showed that, in most cases, they were as socially promising as their classmates.

Clearly, both Jonathan and Lena showed some understanding of the para- meters of encounter, niceness, togetherness, and fighting, and this augurs well for the development of their future friendships. Jonathan's explanation of the encounter sequence involved in a friendship bid proved to be one of the more descriptive accounts of this parameter recorded in interviews. Lena also showed potential for friendships through her applied understanding of the parameters of friendships in her niceness to Monica, a new African-American student and her loyalty and defence of Keshia in a fighting episode with Donna. Herein lies what is arguably the unexhausted finding in this study — the dissonant con- text is not an absolute but a negotiable one. In this regard the findings in the present study overlap with some of the earlier research on the nonsynchronous effects of racial dissonance on children's friendships (Grant, 1984; Schofield,

1981, 1982; Sleeter and Grant, 1986). As Rosenberg (1975) pointed out, the 'dissonant context may have some effects that are positive and others that are negative' (p. 114).

Conclusion

What emerges in this study is that it is imperative for teachers to recognize when some children are making sincere attempts to cultivate their friendships in the face of severe life-situational dissonances. In classrooms where teachers understand that some children are carrying special challenges related to life-situational dissonances, teachers have the potential to facilitate productive social relationships. On the other hand, where there is a lack of understanding of the special needs of children from dissonant contexts, there is the danger that evaluations of the efforts of children like Jonathan, Lena, and Donna could be simplistically based on what are often negative outcomes, rather than on their thwarted attempts to effectively negotiate their friendships.

By drawing attention to the consonant and dissonant features of children's friendships I have attempted to refine the existing theoretical and conceptual focuses on children's friendships in culturally diverse classrooms. I have argued for a nonsynchronous approach that highlights the diffusive and generative nature of early adolescent children's friendships in culturally diverse classrooms. If our understanding of children's friendships in culturally diverse classrooms is to accurately reflect what is really going on there, then we cannot afford to neglect the experiences of children like Jonathan, Lena, and Donna. Further investigations should be directed at investigating how children in other cultur-ally diverse settings negotiate the contingent 'mixes' of life-situational factors in the everyday world of their friendships.

Chapter 5

The Friendly Cultural Stranger as Self-critical Reflexive Narrator

Concepts, like individuals, have their histories and are just as incapable of withstanding the ravages of time as are individuals. But in and through all this they retain a kind of homesickness for the scenes of their childhood. (Kierkegaard, 1965, p. 47)

Well, any nights you want to see anything, I'll take you around. I can take you to the joints — gambling joints — I can take you around to the street corners. Just remember that you are my friend. That's all they need to know. I know these places, and, if I tell them that you're my friend, nobody will bother you. You just tell me what you want to see, and we'll arrange it. (Whyte, 1981, p. 29)

Whyte's (1981) classic study of 'Doc and his boys' in *Street Corner Society* is an exemplar of friendly field relationships in anthropological research. Indeed, Hammersley (1983) wrote that 'Whyte's original still puts most examples of this genre to shame' (p. 4). Readers familiar with Whyte's study know that his friendly field relationships in an Italian-American slum district in the North End of Boston were not so much appropriated but intuitive responses. Friendly field relationships, often quixotic, mercenary, or heart-wrenching, have been well-rehearsed in anthropological writings (Van Maanen, 1988). By one of those paradoxical symmetries that often exist in anthropology, it would seem that the majority of researchers are to paraphrase one of Tennyson's (1870) lines 'one equal temper of friendly hearts,' with few conscientious exceptions (see Peshkin, 1986; Kennedy, 1954). This surprises me. I would have expected more contradictory and nonsynchronous relationships.

The spark for my thinking about my role as a friendly cultural stranger originated with my reading of Powdermaker's classic *Stranger and Friend* (1966). Reflecting on a lifetime of anthropological fieldwork, Powdermaker wrote that the heart of the participant observation method rests not in the dualism, but duality of involvement and detachment. Despite the significant corpus of literature dealing with the topic of involvement and detachment in anthropological research, little self-conscious reflection exists on the part that emotion plays in friendly field relationships.

Two heuristically discrete but interrelated questions guided my reflections:

What friendly field relationships are evidenced in my work? This basic question is anterior, however, to the question that shows the anthropologist as social scientist at work: How do I resolve the tensions between a friendly personal disposition and the multiplicity of roles that I experience in fieldwork. My answers to these questions take up, in turn, the following topics:

1. Rhetorical nuances in the literature on friendly cultural stranger field relationships;
2. Exemplars from my own research studying children's friendships in a fifth-grade culturally diverse class in a public elementary school in Atlanta, Georgia; and
3. Concluding remarks on the friendly cultural stranger as self-critical reflexive narrator.

Moving Beyond Rhetorical Persuasion and Production

The stranger is . . . being discussed here . . . not as the wanderer who comes today and goes tomorrow, but rather as the person who comes today and stays tomorrow. He is, so to speak, the *potential* wanderer . . . The unity of nearness and remoteness involved in every human relation is organized, in the phenomenon of the stranger . . . (Simmel, 1950, p. 402)

The rhetoric of establishing friendly field relationships is interwoven in some of the most celebrated accounts in qualitative research (Malinowski, 1922; Berreman, 1962; Powdermaker, 1966). The 'friendly cultural stranger' is often represented as a generalizable 'social type' (Johnson, 1975) with a predictable coherence of characteristics, centered on establishing 'social comfort' norms, including 'politeness,' 'naivete,' and 'goodwill.' Some historical aspect reminds us that even Malinowski, arguably the most celebrated of all friendly cultural strangers, was described by one of his students at the London School of Economics as a paradox: friendly and helpful as well as cruel and sarcastic (Powdermaker, 1966). Cast in Malinowski's (1929) own words, 'personal friendships encourage spontaneous confidences and the repetition of intimate gossip' (pp. 282–3). This is especially true given that to 'one degree or another,' as Hammersley and Atkinson (1983) suggest, 'the ethnographer will be channeled in line with existing networks of friendship and enmity, territory and equivalent "boundaries"' (p. 73). The principle of *reflexivity* and its navigational challenges were critical in this respect. Atkinson (1980) explained reflexivity in operational terms, as follows:

The ethnographer navigates and explores the varied surface of diverse social scenes: the backwaters as well as the main streams. By virtue of the acts of the transactions he or she engages in, the ethnographer/

reporter recounts the actor's discoveries and self-discoveries. Informants and hosts tell their stories, and in turn the ethnographers have their own tales to tell. (pp. 5–6)

Simmel's 'Stranger'

The hybrid approach that I used to mediate territorial boundaries was derived from literacy and social domains of reality. Simmel's distinction between *intimate form* and *intimate content*, described in his classic book, *The Stranger* (1950), served as a constant reminder of the demarcation of my role as researcher. I set out to maintain content over form. In this distinction content of interaction (for example, secrets) were shared without compromise but when the form of interaction took over one or both of the participants felt that the relationship could potentially become more than a field one. Therefore, my challenge was not to succumb to pretense, on the one hand, or compromise my role, on the other hand.

In his critique of Simmel's writings on sociological distance, Brown (1989) reconciled the oppositional elements in Simmel's *The Stranger* as follows: 'The participant side of participant-observation . . . affords nearness, while the observer side lends farness' (p. 55). A noteworthy coda to this reconciliation of nearness and farness is that it fails if the stranger refuses to leave and confounds the spatial and temporal tensions. While lore and legend surrounding the longevity of certain doctoral research projects exist in all academic contexts, few would argue that the majority of research students want 'to finish and move on.' I was one.

In the study described here, the burden of ethical decisions was more than a theoretical construction; they were personal responses to dilemmas that arose in interpersonal contexts; they fell on my own personal-scientific conscience, and were wrestled with in 'living' experiences. This contrasts with qualitative researchers who often paint themselves in benign unidimensional portraits, with little reflexive sense of what it means to mediate the multiplicity of researcher roles that they encounter in fieldwork. What is needed is a sensitizing, bracketing approach that includes a self-portrait of the researcher, warts and all (making sure, of course, to paint only those warts that are there).

Forster's 'Flat and Round' Characters

Forster's (1927) distinction between 'round' and 'flat' characters served as a complement and counterpoint to Simmel's writings on individuality and social forms. Using the point of view of the stranger, Forster provides a potent example of how communication and human feeling are thwarted in the clash of characters and ideas. Forster used the literary concept of 'round' characters as dominant and integrative character-type projections, with much unpredictability and lack of coherence. In contrast to 'flat' characters who were described as unidimensional, 'round' characters were seen as eschewing a cultural stereotype, and were seen as flexible research bargainers. Two quotes from Forster's *Aspects of the Novel* (1927) will suffice to capture the interplay of 'flat' and 'round' characters. My application of these frames of reference will hopefully become apparent in the remainder of the chapter:

> Flat characters were called 'humours' in the seventeenth century, and are sometimes called types, and sometimes caricatures. In their purest form, they are constructed around a single idea or quality: when there is more than one factor in them, we begin getting the curve towards the round. (p. 104)

> The test of a round character is whether it is capable of surprising in a convincing way. If it does not convince, it is a flat pretending to be round. (p. 118)

Making the Most of Flatness

There is a useful contrastive rhetoric here between friendly cultural strangers who cursorily describe their roles in 'cardboard cut-out' depictions as 'helpers,' 'writers,' and 'aides,' for example, versus those who seriously wrestle with the multiplicity of roles that they experience as problematic.

The previous paragraph is not an argument for totally discarding our 'flat' representations of ourselves. Indeed, 'flat' and ascribed roles have methodological possibilities that I will pursue, briefly. For example, my role as a photographer, like many other researchers before me, helped me to 'speed rapport, involve people in the research, release anecdotes and recollections, so accelerating the sometimes lengthy process of building fieldwork relationships and locating reliable informants' (Walker and Weidel, 1985, p. 213). The point here is that the photographs for the picture-sociometric test on children's friendship choices amounted to frozen 'snapshots' but the light-hearted relief that the picture-taking sessions induced, proved a touchstone in my developing relationships with the participants in my study.

My role as a teacher's aide served similar expeditious functions. I undertook the role of teacher's aide as part of my reciprocation deal with the classroom teacher. It often proved a 'schizophrenic' one. It drew on all my resources to maintain role flexibility in the same classroom space with the children-as-students and the teacher-as-supervisor. The risk of falling into what were often instinctual didactic responses to the teaching and learning situation was ever present when I was working through this role. On the credit side, this role helped me legitimize interaction with the children, often in the slow and easy afternoons when interaction with the children was minimally possible. It also provided opportunities for donning 'the clown's mask' with playful comments and rolling-eye gazes when the teacher's back was turned in another direction.

In this way, the procedural role of teacher's aide contributed much to my repertoire of within-role roles.

Turning Towards Rotundity

Although these roles were generative sources of data, they were not key ones. My concern, as the proceeding pages will unfold, was not with what I was doing, but with 'why,' 'when,' 'where,' and 'how' I was doing what I was supposed to be doing. These self-created 'interrogatives' were directed at peeling back the layers of who I was becoming as a researcher. I found much to reflect on in my researcher log, theoretical memos, and observer comments, notwithstanding worthwhile complications of my own social and cultural identity. The easily recognizable and simple flatness of the aide and photographer stand in contrast to the dominant character-projection of my role as a 'friendly cultural stranger and self-critical reflexive narrator.' The reader is reminded of Forster's test for the round or turn towards rotundity, as I move more deeply into my account.

Combining the ethnographic and literary challenges together required an approach that could potentially describe, interpret, voice, and embody lived emotional experience. The approach that I used was intended to potentially enable the anthropological axiom of a broadly-based holism and its reflexive connection to myself as an anthropologist to emerge. In this way, I hoped to navigate between what Boon (1982) has described as the 'blushless Promethean' approach of Malinowski and his disciples, and contrasting 'fully participating' existential approaches (see Adler and Adler, 1987).

My experiences as a friendly cultural stranger are melted into my first day in the field. Many scenes from my own childhood are woven in and through the unfolding story (see Kierkegaard, 1965, p. 47). The layered account is influenced by Schutz's (1970) writings on *durée*, or stream of consciousness as it naturally flows in lived experience, and by Ronai's more recent rehearsal of it in her examination of a typical 'night in the life of a dancer' (see Ronai, 1992). In doing so, the challenge became reflexive as opposed to tactical; interpretive rather than anecdotal; open on sentiment, but hopefully short on sentimentality. After one of Ronai's (1992) rhetorical strategies, 'three asterisks denote a shift to a different temporal/spatial/attitudinal realm' (p. 102). The multiplicity of possibilities inherent in these realms are focused through the lens of how sense was made between pretense and compromise in my fieldwork experiences.

*   *   *

Entering a school from a side-door always provides you with a unique 'broadside'. Standing like Cortez on the isthmus of Panama, I felt a surge of excitement that I had arrived at the site for my study. Stanley Hazel Elementary School which exuded a well-seasoned ambience was grist for the mill for any would-be semiotician. I was immediately reminded of Jackson's (1968) 'universal smells,' 'orange peels and peanut butter sandwiches,' and 'delicate pungency of children's perspiration' (p. 7). And also reminded of Jackson's claim that 'only when the classroom is encountered under somewhat unusual circumstances, does it appear, for a moment, a strange place filled with objects that command our attention' (1968, p. 115). Quickly the universal smells of the ethnographic present began to mix with the smells of the ethnographic past. These are the particular smells that linger long after they are exhaled. These smells seem strangely fragranted (with detachment) now rather than noxious (with involvement) then. These are the smells from the days when I was truly among schoolchildren in Mr Kildangan's classroom — the smell of the smelly Skellys with the rubber bellies who smelled of the free bun and milk. I can smell their poverty again. And Mr Kildangan, with the mottled inky hands and infamous 'quick-draw' vocational zeal. 'I'm loaded today', he liked to say. I can smell the fear he engendered now. The heavy whiff of chalk dust settles. The visual moment forming.

The ghosts of a convent school education in what is still, arguably, the most culturally homogeneous country in Western Europe were eerily evoked in the little garden courtyards that separated the small cluster of school buildings. A passing teacher informs me that a famous architect built the school. Recess already. I was already 'mining', 'disciplining', and 'taming' biases, as the excited cadences of children's playground voices reminded me of the Opies' (1959, 1969) work on the universality of the lore and language of children's social lives. While I was pondering whether all this familiarity and strangeness could be metaphorically represented as a continuum, pendulum, or, perhaps a spiral, the inevitable 'Can I help you?' echoed from the office end of the tunnel-like hallway. Broadside aborted. I know that school secretaries can hear the grass growing and know how everything works: and promptly, I was clip-clopping with the school secretary down to the principal's office.

Through the gaps in the classroom doors, I could see that Stanley Hazel represented the depth and breadth of diversity that I needed for my study. It not take a major leap of my sociological imagination to realize that I was among a 'strange tribe.' Criterion sampling being processed. 'So you're at Central State, is it?' the secretary inquired, ascribing me the role of college student. I explained my recent history. We were joined by a teacher. Introduced. My 'Irishness' audibly projected in my brogue added some levity to our walk. 'Hasn't he a neat accent!' she exclaimed. Turning more directly to me, she continued, 'I have a friend from Jamaica and she says "how's it go'in," instead of "how're you do'in," just like you do.' Criterion sampling over. Ice broken. Long walk over. The school secretary ushered me into the principal's office.

While I waited for the principal to finish clearing reports, textbooks, and crumbs from his desk, I became momentarily aware that I was having difficulties connecting with the rhythmical relationships of the conversation and the dance down the hallway with the school secretary. I was then reminded of how Jack Kerouac, the beatnik poet, and later Sam Shephard, the playwright, used jazz-sketching with words to convey 'imagery in motion' in their writings. The clip-clopping disappeared around a corner. My conversation with Mr George Craig, the Scots-Irish principal of Stanley Hazel Elementary School was next.

*　　*　　*

Armed with the fresh data from my criterion sampling, I was hoping that this attempt, my fourth, to find a research site would not follow what was becoming a pattern of beguiling welcomes and cordial but hasty farewells. The principal who had been briefed by a colleague on the purpose of my study greeted me as 'the young man that Jeff Wintersmith from Brookstaff called about. English or Irish? I'm Scots-Irish. George Craig's my name.' Not wishing to reenact several chapters of Irish history, I settled for putting forth a simple distinction that focused on demographic contrasts between the Irish and the Scots-Irish (and remained 'mute' on 800 years of agrarian, social, economic, and religious conflict). Later that afternoon driving home in that state of 'virtual reality' that often follows a hard day's observing, I was reminded of what the essayist V.S. Pritchett (1967) described as the natural silence behind the Irishman's wit and passion. Perhaps I was atypical, I mused as the fluorescence of a local convenience store in another sleepy, single-stoplight Georgia town reminded me that I was not only close to home but also twenty miles from where I was living. Amber – Red – Green. Go. I didn't move. Blending the ethnographic present and the ethnographic past is perhaps a dreamy metatheme in my work. Amber – Red – Green. Go. Now.

Yet, the situation with the principal was fraught with uncertainty. Behind the cordial smiles, there was the little matter of my authenticity. 'You know the name Craig? That is C-R-A-I-G?,' he spelled it out biting every sound for clarity. To turn my back abruptly on our common Irish genealogical roots would surely have been the kiss of death, not to mention a breach of 'the intimate cooperation [that] is required,' as Goffman (1959) maintains, 'if a given projected definition of the situation is to be maintained' (p. 104). This episode represented a critical shift in my friendly field relationships from 'unknowingly' to also 'wittingly' projecting my own 'Irishness.' There were other occasions when elements of our common romantic and heritage culture provided us with unexhausted sources of conversation on our armchair journeys to Killarney. Often I wondered if I should shatter the postcard-perfect image of yellowing straw-thatched cottages, crooked chimneys and faint curling smoke redolent in his romantic descriptions. Untangling the 'terrible beauty' of Irish affairs was never canceled, only postponed.

These experiences contrast sharply with those of a fellow countryman of mine and erstwhile friendly cultural stranger. In his study of Afro-Caribbean and Asian students in an inner-city (Kilby) comprehensive school in what was officially regarded as one of Britain's main black 'problem' areas, Mac an Ghaill (1988) found his 'Irishness' as enabling as I found mine, but for different reasons. For the students in his study, he was 'Irish not white,' and therefore could be trusted. Contrasting with the essentially romantic and heritage dimensions of my acceptance, his was based on immediate political and cultural factors. While obvious differences exist, the stories serve as bold claims of the potentially diffusive quality of Irish origins in facilitating entrée and establishing rapport on two sides of the Atlantic. Perhaps, there are others 'out there,' who can provide complements and counterpoints to these claims.

*   *   *

Convenient attacks of blindness or deafness (Hargreaves, 1967, pp. 203–4) suffused with sympathetic gazes (Fine and Sandstrom, 1988, p. 58) paradoxically resulted in trust and respect in my friendly field relationships with the fifth-grade participants in my study. The die was cast early when Alvin, an African-American male, finished his running burst from the lunchroom back into the classroom (a flagrant breach of the school code of discipline and management) with the telling quip: '[yours truly] ain't gonna do nothin,' he ain't a teacher.' The diplomatic tables did not stop spinning thereafter.

Name-calling was a recurring feature of the children's racist taunts and innuendos. Like voices on the wind, taunts of 'Cambodian fool,' 'Ching Chong,' 'Jalapeno,' 'Jungle person,' and 'Nigger' were difficult to pin down. It is so different when you are listening with children's ears rather than feebly bending adult ears to hear what children are hearing. I was truly among schoolchildren when I heard the loud whispers for the smelly Skellys with the rubber bellies. 'The smelly Skellys!' 'The smelly Skellys!' 'The smelly Skellys with the rubber bellies, nah — nah — nanah — nah, nah — nanah — nahnah, Nah!'

Sitting in the natural amphitheater of the school's music room, children's increasing breaching of previously taboo subjects were evident in simulated 'mooning,' chants of 'Here comes Johnny,' and classroom gossip about Lena, a 13-year-old African-American female, the oldest student in the class. Her reputational bias fuelled rumors of her purported pregnancy. Nantoba, an African-American male, explained that the boys were saying that Lena was 'overweighted' and therefore 'pregnant.' The substitute teacher 'fiddled' hopelessly with scratchy records on an old record player and the children showed some of their secret world but realized that they would not be compromised in the company of two 'friendly strangers.' This was a rare peek into the culture of childhood that Opie and Opie (1959) describe as 'not intended for adult ears . . . at once more real, more immediately serviceable, and vastly more entertaining than anything which they learn from grown-ups' (p. 1). I watched. He fiddled. And the children played for a fleeting half-hour.

*　　*　　*

In my introduction to the children, I described myself as a writer interested in children's social lives in American schools. This piece of esoteria lasted surprisingly long, but was blatantly foiled by the unintended irony of Kai, a Cambodian male, who innocently remarked that after six months, 'It must be long paper, if you're still here.' Later at recess on my first morning, Alvin, Nantoba, and Montrel, all African-American males, stated and asked, 'You're from Mexico, speak Spanish.' Turning this experience over in my mind, I concluded that, whereas the children had a misconception of my identity, it was not necessarily a negative one. Out of this experience, I cultivated an 'innocent abroad' variant of the much used 'naive adult approach' in qualitative inquiry with young children. This enabled me to ask rudimentary questions about African-American jewelry, computer games, and the rules of football and jump-rope. It also allowed me to meander around the playground and loiter on some inane pretext with the boys in the vicinity of the wrestling mats or spark a conversation with the girls while standing under the 'shade tree' (like many others to get respite from the noonday Georgia sun), avoiding the inquisitorial stance that often haunts adult researchers working in children's social worlds.

In these settings, I would discover that a less romantic version of 'Irishness' was emerging through the medium of the pen-pal letter exchange that I had arranged with fifth-grade children in an Irish primary school. 'They eat pizza, don't they?' 'Are U2 Irish?' 'What is Sinéad O'Connor really like?' 'Does Rory have Super Mario?' These questions tested much about who I was becoming socially and culturally in the heat and light of a changing Ireland. And Schutz's (1962) reminder that neither the homecomer's self nor his home are ever the same once he has travelled away, was clear.

Ways of the Self-critical Reflexive Narrator — Searching for One's 'Own' Social and Cultural Identity

Success in the art of fieldwork depends, to a considerable extent, on establishing a very special role that legitimizes a kind of information-getting behavior that was not previously part of the social expectations within the community. They may identify with local inhabitants, . . . but the role of gatherer of information, persistent questioner and stranger from another culture is always part of one's social identity. (Pelto and Pelto, 1973, p. 182)

Recently, some anthropologists have begun to critique the arbitrariness and convenience of the friendly cultural stranger role, citing the importance of recognizing the unique and contingent 'mix' of abilities, needs, capacities, interests, and demands inherent in this claim (see Brice Heath, 1993; Fine, 1993). Few would argue, nevertheless, that laying bare fieldwork methods in an autobiographical way is a *sine qua non* for all qualitative researchers. But clearly those who follow the road more travelled need to move beyond *post scriptum* fieldwork accounts to ones that demystify the anthropologist as a social scientist at work.

Any approach for challenging commonly held assumptions concerning friendly fieldwork relationships must be open to the development of the self, while recognizing that such a commitment includes methodological and rhetorical conventions. Ample cautions against mixing the ethnographic and the literary exist (Bulmer, 1984). Contrasting with Atkinson's (1990) writings on *rapproachment* between the social and literary domains of reality, potent as they are in their own right, this paper goes beyond concerns about rhetorical persuasion and production. It challenges the traditional dualism that has failed to consider friendly cultural strangers as medium and outcome of the action that they recursively organize in 'living' fieldwork.

The issue of combining the ethnographic and literary domains of reality is more fundamental than whether to provide a 'methodological appendix' or separate paper, as some methodological sword-play between Assinck and Brice Heath in a recent paper, 'Reflections from the Field,' *Anthropology and Education Quarterly*, **24**, 3, pp. 249–68, reveals. Demystification of the anthropologist's role is to a great extent the essence of ethnographic writing; it flexes the ethnographic imagination and finds expression in the textual constructions of reality. This reflection represents a unique and contingent 'mix' of subtleties and intangibilities in the 'ordinary' experiences of one particular friendly cultural stranger. It suggests that making theoretical and methodological decisions with reference to social and cultural identities has relevance for self-critical reflexivity, in anthropological research, most notably one's 'own' social and cultural identity.

Chapter 6

An Inquiry Approach for Investigating Children's Friendships with Student Teachers in a School–University Partnership

Like Picasso, teacher researchers are heading a revolution in modern art — the modern art of teaching. We are looking at research possibilities from new angles. We are redefining our roles, rejecting the small and impoverished models of research that attempt to turn classroom inquiry into a pseudo-scientific horse race. (Atwell, 1991, quoted in Hubbard and Power, 1993, p. xvi)

Wait till you see what we're up to! (Hubbard and Power, 1993, p. xvii)

These quotations, culled from Hubbard and Power's book *The Art of Classroom Inquiry: A Handbook for Teacher Researchers* (1993), cut to the heart of the challenges and spirit of renewal inherent in teacher research. Much has been written in praise of teacher research (see Bissex and Bullock, 1987; Goswami and Stillman, 1987; Hubbard and Brown, 1993), but little has been written about student-teacher research (see Cochran-Smith, 1991). What if the same opportunities for doing action research existed for 'working student teachers'? There is nothing in this challenge that is necessarily outside the realm of possibilities for beginning professional teachers in teacher education preparation programs?

Avoiding the invidious traps of 'pseudo-scientific horseracing', globs of unintelligible data, and the failure to make connections with 'real world' pedagogical practices are pervasive threats in all fieldwork projects. These concerns put in fundamental terms 'how,' 'why,' and 'for whom' we should pursue all meaningful research activity. The existence of so many school–university partnerships dedicated to the renewal of teaching and the education of educators (Goodlad, 1994) would appear to be a logical context for incorporating action research into student teachers' everyday beginning professional experiences. There is clearly a common-sense argument for 'getting started' early.

In this chapter, I describe a comprehensive action research process that student teachers used to investigate children's friendships. The plan follows Marsh's (1992) four fundamental processes or 'moments' for developing a *plan* of action, *acting* to implement the plan, *observing* the effects of action in the context in which it happens, and *reflecting* on these effects as a basis for further planning and a succession of cycles (pp. 117–18). It is not intended as the definitive process, nor necessarily the appropriate one for all contexts. It is, instead, presented as an example of the challenges inherent in foregrounding children's friendships as a pivotal concern in doing action research with student teachers. This chapter is loosely organized with reference to three convenient chronological phases of the project, and the integral themes and strands of the four moments of planning, acting, observing, and reflecting.

Aspect

The action research project was collaboratively undertaken, planned, carried through, and reflected upon by 27 student teachers (26 female, 1 male; all European-American) and the writer, in an alternative early childhood education undergraduate teacher education program. The program is a major component in a school–university partnership which is currently underway at The University of Georgia and in local education settings (see Allexsaht-Snider, Deegan, and White, 1995).

The program is premised on the salient themes of multiculturalism, constructivism, reflectivity, and technology, related integral concepts (for example, child-centeredness, choice, integration), applied methods of teaching (for example, whole language, cooperative learning), and students teachers' 'real world,' field experiences in one urban, and two rural Georgia public elementary schools.

The children's friendships project was designed as a combined class and field requirement in an early childhood education course, 'Ourselves and Children as Learners.' This course examined beginning student teachers' own memorable learning experiences in public and private elementary school classrooms, mainly in the southeastern United States, in the early 1980s. These remembrances served as ways of connecting with the complexities of children's social learning in the present culture of public elementary schools.

Research questions were reflexively derived from students own experiences in the field. Data collection included observation, interview, and sociometric procedures. Data were analyzed using a speculative form of classifying and categorizing major insights (Davies, 1982). Throughout the project, I served as an *external facilitator* (Marsh, 1992), acting as 'sounding board' or as 'critical friend' (Ebutt and Partington, 1982) in helping to widen perspectives, clarify ideas, and lend support when needed. It is suggested that this chapter should be read with close reference to the following companion chapter which contains the final project reports of two student teachers.

The Project

As the college teacher for the early childhood education teacher education introductory course on learning and teaching strategies, I was able to set the stage for the project. In the beginning weeks of the course, we read Paley's *White Teacher* (1989) as an exemplar of how the interactive complexities of constructivism, multiculturalism, and reflectivity can be meaningfully problematized in current early childhood education pedagogical discourse. Our discussions of Paley's (1989) book helped create a context for situating the topic of children's friendships as a potentially worthwhile and engaging one for the student teachers first action research project.

I began with a simple think/pair/share protocol in which students briefly reflected with their seating patterns, and later with the class as a whole, on the temporal, spatial, and attitudinal features of their own positive and negative memorable friendships in classrooms and schools. The students began taking their first steps towards questioning the tacit and taken-for-granted surfaces of the etiology of their own friendships as complex phenomena. Their fading memories of the interests, concerns, rituals, routines, activities, and values inherent in their own friendships provided a compelling rationale for problematizing popular notions of children's friendships, most notably, their 'own' popular notions.

Following this cursory introduction aimed at problematizing and legitimizing the grounded nature of the project, the students set off to see what it might be like to be and have friends on the playgrounds of the three program schools in the local area, one urban, the other two rural. The playground was selected as the place for investigation because it can potentially provide a highly developed instance of wrestling with involvement and detachment when researching children's social lives. It is especially challenging for student teachers who typically have a natural desire to be 'friendly,' but who do not necessarily want to intellectualize the experience, and destroy the magic of it all, as they see it. In an effort to privilege the grounded focus of the project, the introduction did not include any reference to recent and relevant research on children's friendships. Readings were introduced later following the collection of data and preliminary data analyses in Phase 3 of the project.

Phase 1

The student teachers began Phase 1 of the project with a visit to the playgrounds of their assigned program schools. The duration of the visit coincided with varying scheduled recess periods across the three schools. The average recess period lasted, weather permitting, approximately 15 minutes. Some cooperating teachers extended recess to 30 minutes in order to provide the student teachers with a 'decent' block of time for observations.

This visit was the student teachers first to the school and helped provide introductory glimpses of the children. The purpose of the visit was to observe the children in highly developed instances of play and friendships, rather than in the context of the typical formal 'first meeting' in assigned classroom. The

---

Table 6.1:   Children's Friendships Project Workbook 1

- *Getting* Ready
  Before the children in your class go out for recess, construct a blank map of the 'empty' playground (clipboard, writing paper, watch, and color pens etc., will be helpful).
- *On the Playground*
  1. Fill in your map of the playground. (Use the map as a working guide — scratch arrows, circles, or whatever symbols that will help you make sense of what is happening).
  2. List 3–5 activities that are occurring.
  3. List 3–5 behaviors that are occurring.
  4. Identify groupings (pairs, triads, or other combinations).
  5. Outline the dynamics of disputes and fighting.
  6. Are there any situations where race, ethnicity, gender, class, disability or other features seem to be critical?
  7. Record any verbal or nonverbal communication that you are hearing or observing.
  8. Before leaving the playground write out a number of emerging insights in bullet form.
- *Understanding your Playground Observations*
  1. Color code the various groupings. Make a key for comparing dyads, triads, or other groupings.
  2. Using #1–8 (or whatever combination you ended up with), write a two-page narrative report of your observations. The narrative should answer this question: What did you see happening and what do you think it meant for the children involved (includes what kind of learning was going on)? Title your report with a metaphor that you think captures the essence of your observations.
- *Preparations for Phase 2*
  1. Write down 3–5 focus questions based on things that interested you and that you would like to follow up on in Phase 2.
  2. Write down 3–5 strengths in your data collection approach.
  3. Write down 3–5 changes that you would make in your data collection approach for Phase 2.
  4. Write down the changes (if any) in the way that you intend relating to children and adults when you are collecting data in Phase 2.

prefield visit was ostensibly intended as a dress rehearsal for the 'real thing' which followed a week later.

A *Children's Friendships Project Workbook 1* was designed and rehearsed with the student teachers. It was designed to help the students grapple with the challenges of studying children's friendships on the playground 'from the other side' children's. The prefield visit was intended to help student teachers establish some sense of direction for what they were going to do more systematically during their field experience, and to establish purposeful research questions and concerns. The log included guided procedural processes for studying the complexities of children's friendships during the concentrated period of recess time on the playground (see Table 6.1).

All students received individual feedback on their narrative reports at the end of Phase 1 of the project. The section aimed at eliciting student responses about their preparations for Phase 2 of the project was the central focus in my

Table 6.2:   Response to student teachers' narrative reports at the end of Phase 1 of the project

- *Make Friendships Central*
  The project is not about everything and anything that children do on playgrounds. It is about children's friendships. What light do activities, behaviors, and situations throw on the central topic of children's friendships? Put simply, what are you learning about children's friendships and how are you going about this work?
- *Friendships are Unique*
  Friendships are unique — they are not just another way of saying children play with each other in peer groups. They are special close friendships. Find out the key aspects of children's friendships — how they get started, how children negotiate them on a daily basis, how they break up, and what comes after the breakup. Sometimes, fights, disputes, arguments, group size connect with friendships.
- *See Points on the Landscape*
  You can't see everything and make sense of it. Pick a 'space' on the playground landscape (a space where friendships are happening) and like a good artist or photographer zoom in on a specific time, event, or person(s). Using the metaphor of the photographer, take pictures from different angles and distances.
- *Hear Children's Voices*
  What are children saying between and among themselves — let's hear their voices and not your voice over on what they are saying. Plan on being a good listener. Figure out how you are going to get within earshot, without compromising the quality of your data.
- *Keep Data Organized*
  Dates, times, places should be placed on all data collected. Make sure to keep clean copies of maps ready if you have a highly active playground with lots of kids. Also key your map.
- *Work Data into Daily Narratives*
  Get children's voices into your end-of-the-day narratives. What exactly did they say in their own words about their own social worlds. Block out time and write up your emerging insights.
- *Work Data More and More*
  Do not tack on a piece of data everyday — integrate what you saw on Tuesday with what you are seeing on Wednesday. Create a quilt rather than build a brick house with data.
- *Seek Disconfirming Evidence*
  As you collect data, it will become clear that some things do not fit in with the key themes that are emerging in your fieldwork. Follow up these disconfirming evidences. Do not throw away things that do not fit easily because they can tell you so much about your own biases and prejudices. Good observers are not squeaky clean and they need to share their own limitations.

responses to the students. I responded to the salient recurring substantive and procedural challenges that all students had discussed in their narrative reports in an open memo which was later discussed in class (see Table 6.2).

Between Phase 1 and Phase 2, I also covered some practical in-class assignments on separating observations from inferences and value judgments. Florio-Ruane's (1990) work on creating classroom case studies proved a useful source for helping student teachers make distinctions between inferences and judgments in instructional contexts, and a useful springboard for class discussions on how students might have misconceived some of these distinctions

---

Table 6.3:   Constructing a sociogram

- Each child could be asked, confidentially, to write down the names of the three people with whom they would most like to play.
- Also each child could be asked to write down the names of the three children with whom they would least like to play.
- This data could be used to map patterns of friendship.
- Where choices are positively reciprocated, connect the names with a bi-directional arrow (i.e., <----->).
- Where the choice is not reciprocated, connect the names with a uni-directional arrow (i.e., ----->).
- Where a negative choice is reciprocated (mutual dislike), connect the names with disconnected arrows (i.e., <-- --- -->).
- Where a negative choice is one-way, connect the names with a broken arrow (i.e., -- --- -- --->).
- Features that could emerge include:
  — Clusters — three or more pupils who show mutual, positive relationships (cliques).
  — Pairs — two pupils who show mutual choices.
  — Isolates — those who no one positively chooses but towards whom no one displays negative feelings.
  — Rejectees — those who are negatively identified and actively disliked.
- Final construction step is the generation of questions that focus topics for further investigation.

---

in Phase 1 of the project. Additionally, Hubbard and Power's (1993) basic guidelines for the use of sociograms was introduced as a way of establishing frequency and pattern of contact between and among children on the playground. A more involved sociogram based on Pollard and Tann's (1987) approach for revealing children's own perspectives on their friendship patterns was introduced in response to some student teachers' requests for more structured and descriptive frames of reference for analyzing children's friendships (see Table 6.3). A variant of Pollard and Tann's (1987) approach was used by Meredith Gaskill, one of the students teachers, whose final narrative report follows in the next chapter.

Phase 2

For Phase 2, I prepared a *Children's Friendships Project Workbook 2*. The second workbook was designed to provide guided help for developing and expanding the themes that student teachers had identified for further study in their narrative field reports at the end of Phase 1 of the project (see Table 6.4). The second workbook rehearsed some of the preliminaries from Phase 1. It also introduced the concept of role negotiation as a pivotal feature of the project, and emphasized strategies for continually searching for basic social processes in the accumulating data bank (see Table 6.5). The workbook format for Days 1 through 5 followed the same daily pattern (see Table 6.6).

Throughout the fieldwork component of the project, I attempted to maintain

Table 6.4:   Children's Friendships Project Workbook 2

- *Getting Ready*
  1.   Research Questions
       Based on your pre-field visit write out 3–5 focus questions that will guide your next round of playground observations.
  2.   Role
       Decide how you are going to enter and establish rapport with children on the playground.
  3.   Equipment
       You will need a blank map of the 'empty' playground. Make several blank copies. A clipboard, writing paper, watch, and color pens could be useful.
- *On the Playground*
  1.   Fill in your map of the playground. Use the map as a working guide — scratch arrows, circles, or whatever symbols that will help you make sense of what is happening.
  2.   List behaviors that are occurring.
  3.   List activities that are occurring.
  4.   Identify groupings (pairs, triads, or any other combinations).
  5.   Outline the dynamics of disputes and fighting.
  6.   Are there any situations where race, ethnicity, gender, class, disability, or other features seem to be critical?
  7.   Record any verbal or nonverbal communications that you are hearing or observing.
  8.   Record any artifacts used by children (for example, toys, cards).
  9.   Before leaving the playground write out a number of emerging insights in bullet form.
- *Reflecting on your Playground Observations*
  1.   Color code the various groupings. Make a key for comparative reference on Day 2.
  2.   Using #1–9 above, write a brief narrative of your observations.
  3.   Refine your focus questions. Clearly write out 3–5 questions for Day 2. You might like to zoom in on particular behaviors, groups, friendships, or other key recurring features. Make some methodological revisions based on the glitches that occurred on Day 1 (for example, role mediation, use of equipment, where you need to be to get the data).

regular contact by visiting the school playgrounds; making telephone calls to principals, cooperating teachers, and student teachers; and sending e-mail communications in response to questions and concerns. These means of communication were intended to provide guidelines for continually searching for what mattered most in the fieldwork projects, and to assist with suggestions for marshalling emerging data, or what students referred to as the 'tons of stuff that I am getting.' An example of an e-mail communication requesting clarity on a methodological and conceptual concern, will be included in one the student teacher reports in Chapter 7.

Phase 3

In Phase 3 of the project, students were asked to synthesize and write up their findings. Prior to the write-up phase, and on completion of data analysis,

Table 6.5: Guidelines for continually working data in Days 2–5

- *Ongoing Data Collection*
  1. Refine your questions and narrow your focus.
  2. Construct maps, sociograms, noting routines, rituals, and activities. Do not spend all your time mapping, get on with observing.
  3. Write one-page narratives on your emerging themes, noting more closely the interplay of cultural features (for example, race, ethnicity, gender, class, disability, and community).
  4. Integrate the 'language of the playground' in your narrative accounts.
  5. Check off what 'you are seeing' versus 'what you expected to see'.
  6. Keep trying to make sense of your observations by looking closely at things that seem out of place, inconsistent, strange, or not as you would have expected.
- *Writing-Up Phase (Post-field Phase)*
  1. Construct a composite map of the playground, illustrating the key themes that emerged during the week. Make a color key that emerged during the week.
  2. Write a 3–5 page final narrative, elaborating the key themes with specific examples and quotive data. Finish the narrative with suggestions for practice and further study. Before the Writing-up Phase, you will be given some readings that will help you relate your grounded findings to the literature on children's playground cultures.

Table 6.6: Example of workbook format for Days 1–5

- Map for the Day
- Observational Notes for the Day
- Sociogram for the Day
- Narrative of Emerging Insights and Focus Questions for the Next Day
- Map for the Next Day with Emerging Themes

the students were introduced to selected theoretical, conceptual, and applied research on children's friendships in mainstream and diverse elementary schools and classrooms. These readings included whole, or portions, of the following publications:

CORSARO, W.A. and EDER, D. (1990) 'Children's peer cultures', *Annual Review of Sociology*, **16**, pp. 197–220.

DEEGAN, J.G. (1993) 'Children's friendships in culturally diverse classrooms', *Journal of Research in Childhood Education*, **7**, 2, pp. 91–101.

POLLARD, A. (1985) *The Social World of the Primary School*, London, Holt, Rinehart and Winston.

SLUCKIN, A. (1981) *Growing up in the Playground*, London, Routledge and Kegan Paul.

The students submitted their final project papers after a few weeks reflection, some shared thoughts on pre-writing, post-field group reflections in class, and the final write-up. Two student teachers' final project papers follow in Chapter 7 as examples of process, product, and spiralling ideas for future action researching about learning and learning about action researching in their ongoing teacher education preparation program, and possibly later.

Two Student Teachers' Beginning Professional Stories of Studying Children's Friendships

This chapter acts as companion chapter for Chapter 6, and is introduced here with a few prefatory comments. Suffice to say, that these two student teachers' stories were selected for inclusion here because they are representative of the student teachers who most wholeheartedly engaged in their first action research project on children's friendships. They also represent illustrative examples of the substantive and methodological challenges of the group as a whole.

Mixing Personal and Professional Stories of Experience

Findings, generally, indicated that student teachers were 'mixing' stories of personal and professional experiences (Connelly and Clandinin, 1990) in the field with a strong intuitive sense of a variety of narrative inquiry styles. Student teachers described how they used role mediation in gaining entrée to their settings, negotiated with key informants, resolved ethical dilemmas concerning confidentiality and anonymity, made decisions concerning discrepant findings, struggled with the vagaries of data collection with 'spring fever' in the air, and attempted to interpret data for an audience that included their peers, university faculty, and practicing teachers.

Embedded in these stories are many oft-cited practical and technical rationales for doing action research, such as the twin and interrelated development of a shared learning process and the creation of a public research product. Admittedly, only time will tell if these fledgling projects can act as spurs towards more emancipatory research efforts (see Marsh, 1992, p. 118). What marks these student teachers' stories apart from the maelstrom of personal and professional stories of experiences which have been published in recent years is threefold. These student teachers' stories provide evidence of the following:

1. A keen inquiring sense of classroom social processes, well in advance of having full responsibility for their own classrooms;
2. Rigorous and relevant experiences working through basic methodological procedures towards fresh insights about learning; and

3. A beginning integrative understanding of the salience of social processes in educational renewal and development programs.

Clusters, Bonds, Fights, and Secrets

Ben Lauricella

The playground is an exciting world. It is a world of freedom. It is filled with best friends, bullies, and those with whom children don't come in contact much. The playground is a dynamic place. The terrain can be a meadow in the middle of some woods where forts and streams can be found or a fenced-in blacktop where basketball hoops and stickball games abound. Each child brings a life experience necklace. On this necklace are many jewels. Some are different languages. Some are different family backgrounds. Some are different racial identities. Some are different religious ideas. Some are different hobbies and interests. Some are body sizes and shapes. There are many other kinds of jewels. No two jewels are the same, and over time, each jewel is polished to a beautiful luster or blemished to dull opaqueness.

Challenges

My time on the playgrounds of 'Central Elementary School' (all personal and place names are fictitious) revealed the intensity of kindergartners' social lives. In only one week, I formed many questions quickly with the help of the teacher and her aide. Yet, as soon as one question was answered, two new ones would surface. There were other challenges in gathering very probing data.

First, kindergartners who only have fifteen minutes to play don't tend to stay in one place for very long. Having all of that natural energy and curiosity also tends to make them frequently change activities. For example, I rarely got the time to listen to Wesley, Tylor Smith, Tylor Bradshaw, and Antonio because they were constantly running to and fro, even though they often remained together.

Second, the world of secrets and exclusivity tended to keep me locked out of their play, especially in the beginning. I will discuss this 'culture of secrets' later. Next, and almost the opposite of being locked out, was the fact that I was a male adult in their midst and actually drew the kids to me, just like iron to a magnet. Once the kids were flocked around me, it was pretty hard to gather data in the same way as someone who is unnoticed and ignored. In this case, their play was not focused towards other children. It was focused towards me. Catching kids in their 'natural element' was very difficult. Another aspect which challenged my data collection were the physical dimensions of the playground.

Third, the time factor was a critical element which hindered my ability to gather revealing data. This contrasts with Deegan (1993) who conducted a long-term study over much of the school year, doing interviews in October, January, and March. I did manage to start formulating some creative concepts about children's friendships at the end of the week, so I can only imagine what marvelous insights I might have obtained and cultivated had I been with the class since the fall. Additional data on children's friendships were also gathered in the classroom setting with the help of Mrs Hollister, the classroom teacher, and her aide, Ms Edgar.

Hispanic Clustering

During a prefield experience visit to Central Elementary School, I noticed that Mario, Teresa, Carlos, and Hannah, the Hispanic children in my class, tended to join a cluster made up of the majority of the Hispanic children from the other kindergarten classes. These children would pick a certain 'spot' as their activity base. During the prefield visit, the cluster was centered in the shade of a large tree in another playground. During my week-long field experience the swing set usually marked the spot. From this base, they would occasionally break off in dyads or triads and go to some other area of the playground, and then return at a later time. I was curious as to whether this all-Hispanic clustering was due to the obstacles created by the language barrier. The teacher, Mrs Hollister, stated that the language barrier was certainly a major factor in limiting the quantity and quality friendships with the English-speaking children.

Perhaps Hannah and Carlos were good examples of this theme of language negotiation. Hannah, the daughter of a Mexican immigrant father, spoke English fairly well, and had a good grasp of many American colloquialisms. This opened many opportunities for her. Reflecting on Deegan's (1993) notion that 'encounters' and 'togetherness' are major elements of consonance (that is, the development of friendships within the children's own accepted parameters for friendships), I saw that Hannah's proficiency with the English language and American culture helped her to be less inhibited around the African-American and European-American children. It also helped her to share feelings in more sophisticated ways about abstract concepts. Interestingly, it was easier for her to 'be nice' with others and, as I observed later, easier for her to fight with others.

Carlos knew the least English of the Spanish-speaking children in the class; yet he was still quite energetic and outgoing, especially around the other Hispanic children. Yet, when he was in the classroom setting, where the Hispanic clustering did not exist for the most part, Carlos was usually in an isolated circumstance, either reading a book alone, playing with magnets alone, or working on the computer alone. Of course, I observed that Carlos did become involved in certain positive social events, such as repeating the stories during story time and helping Antonio and Hardie build things in the 'blocks center.' The classroom teacher also stated that he had gradually showed some mastery of the English language over the school year.

A question of mine, one which was closely related to Deegan's (1993) 'immigrant dissonance' theme, was whether some of this clustering and isolation was forced, not self chosen. This was difficult to answer because I heard no non-Hispanic children actually make derogatory comments, or verbalize any common misconceptions. In fact, many of the non-Spanish-speaking children showed eagerness to make new connections by learning how to count in Spanish and how to say 'Thank you.' For example, at the lunch table, Teresa asked me if I knew how to count to fifteen in Spanish. I began to count, when, suddenly, Julia said, 'I know! Uno, dos, tres, cuatro . . .' Julia looked at Teresa with an expectant gaze. Teresa smiled at me and told Julia, 'Yeah, that's right.' While I was at the 'puzzles center' table, Carlos gave me a puzzle piece which I needed. 'Thank you,' I replied. Mamie, who sat next to Carlos, turned to me and said, 'Carlos said that "Thank you" is "Gracias."'

Mario and Teresa both spoke English at a level conducive for meaningful social interactions. Still, Teresa was more inhibited and, therefore, not quite as fully involved in the Hispanic or American English-speaking clusters. Her pensiveness may have been due to just being a shy child, or due to her family dynamics and, quite possibly, combined family and personal problems. Mario was well accepted by all groups, though he associated mostly with the Hispanic cluster because he showed greater comfort when speaking Spanish.

Speaking Spanish Helps Create Bonds

I came to the conclusion that being more fluent might definitely help me to develop trust and friendship with the children because I came into the classroom and playground with a beginner's level of mastery with Spanish. I believe Teresa helped me realize this most.

Throughout the prefield experience visit and the field experience, Teresa and I played a 'vocabulary game.' The first round happened on the first day of the prefield visit when she asked quite frankly, 'Do you know what "sandia" means?' 'No, do you?' I replied (Fieldnotes for Prefield Visit). Teresa looked at me for a second and shook her head, 'No.' I was determined to find out what that word meant so that I could tell her during the full week experience. A good friend of mine told me that 'sandia' meant 'watermelon.' I asked her later, 'Does it mean "watermelon"?' She laughed and said, 'Yes!' She obviously knew that this was a game (Fieldnotes for Day 1). We played the 'watermelon game' all week. I learned how to say 'butterfly,' 'ice cream,' and many other words which pertained to things we talked about or saw everyday.

More and more, as the week went on, she would smile at me and begin to ask questions which were on her mind, like 'How many cents are there in a dollar?' (Fieldnotes for Day 3) or 'What is the day today?' (Fieldnotes for Day 4). She began to hold my hand more and, as discretely as possible, followed me around the playground. Whenever I turned around, she would be there, smiling.

Fights

Throughout the course of the first three days, I noticed that there were no real fights or full-blown verbal melées. This somewhat surprised me because many of the children came from violent communities. Neither did I observe much play which reflected some sort of gang behavior or violent crime. Perhaps I was reflecting uncritically on what I had read about the effects of violent communities on children's play and development in 'war zones' in large urban contexts in the United States.

Then it happened. On Thursday, during the first recess, I was observing a large group of children playing hopscotch near the music trailer (Fieldnotes for Day 4). I noticed something peculiar about Hannah's behavior. She seemed to be conversing in somewhat louder tones than usual. What really got to me was that, no matter who it was that seemed to be next in line to go, Hannah had to give that person some sort of unspoken permission to proceed. It did not seem to matter if that child was black, white, or Hispanic. It did not seem to matter whether the child was a boy or girl. They were all subject to the same judgment process. Hannah seemed to be the 'gatekeeper.' If any given child did not meet her 'approval,' she simply pushed that person aside with a stiff upper lip, but with no other visible signs of anger or hostility. This occurred for about five minutes, then something else began to stir at the end of the line.

The kids must have begun to grow restless because of Hannah's 'bossiness,' often telling her that they could go if they wanted to. Mamie and Susie, usually a close pair, even began to bump into each other. I looked down to jot down a few notes. As soon as I did, Mamie was on the ground and holding her knee. She said to Susie, 'Why'd you do that?' and began to cry. Susie's face showed that she really did not mean to do it.

Mamie ran over to Mrs Hollister and retold the story, blaming Susie, and also telling how her knee hurt. Mrs Hollister looked at her knee and sighed, 'Mamie, you can sit down and miss recess if it hurts that bad.' Mamie rubbed her knee and seemed to think for a second. 'It's not so bad.' 'Susie, did you knock Mamie down?' asked Mrs Hollister. Susie nodded her head and apologized to Mamie. They quickly hugged each other and returned to the hopscotch area.

What I realized about these two incidents was that Hannah's actions seemed to go unchecked for the most part and that Susie and Mamie seemed to find clarity in a third party, Mrs Hollister. Then I reflected for a while. Hannah was a minority female student. Maybe her outgoing, dominating personality, combined with her fluency with English and the surprise element of it all allowed this 'gatekeeper' behavior to continue for such a long time during one game sequence.

In Susie's and Mamie's case, they immediately went to an adult third party when confusion or turmoil appeared, possibly looking for some 'mediator/ negotiator.' It was obvious that Mamie played the role of 'decision maker/ leader' for the pair. Mrs Hollister noted that Susie was big for her grade level and that she had stayed back for one year. She also noted that Susie was not always in complete command of her dexterity/motor skills. By acting as 'the mediator,' Mrs Hollister helped the two girls clarify friendship, concerns, interests, and values, and keep uppermost a key factor — that the children were close friends.

Secrets

Hardie truly turned me on to the whole idea of secrets while we were talking on the playscape. He asked me, 'Do you want to see a secret place where I go?' I replied that I did. He then thought for a second and said to me, 'Maybe I'll show you the most secreted place.' He lead me to a very secret little nook, guarded by boards. A 'culture of secrets' exists among children. I really picked up on this with three groups of friends.

The first group was Colin and Chad. They shared a common friendship interest in unique rocks and insects. Whenever I got close enough to ask them what they where discussing, they would see me and move somewhere else. Their favorite 'spot' was underneath the corner of the big playscape. Antonio, Wesley, and Miah never stood still. Yet, when I did approach them, they dispersed or confronted me individually. They seemed to chase each other around a lot and laugh together a great deal.

The last group was Rosemary, Stephanie (a friend from the other kindergarten class), and Emma. Their secret place was the 'oak tree corner.' Their shared interest was only revealed after I did some spying. I sat behind a tree and looked the other way, pretending not to notice what the girls were doing. On earlier occasions, when I had openly approached them, they responded by running away. This time, I heard Emma say, 'It's almost done. Just a few more things to build.'

They went off to look for some sticks, then suddenly Emma saw me and asked, 'Do you want to see our crystal garden?' I replied that I did. Rosemary overheard this conversation and quickly confronted Stephanie. 'Why did you tell him?,' she demanded. Stephanie had leaked the secret plans, and Rosemary was clearly not pleased.

When I related this story to Mrs Hollister, she noted that this common occurrence might be the children's attempt to empower themselves based on the privileged information of the crystal garden. The privilege was not the garden, so much, but the secret. The secret could refer to some hidden club or hangout like 'oak tree corner' or it could refer to some secret interest, like rocks, insects, and crystal gardens.

When I have a chance to do further research and observe children's everyday behaviors in and out of the classroom, I will certainly pursue how young children from different cultures perceive each other at the primary grade levels. I would also like to explore the impact of the 'forgiveness factor' (the ability to quickly strengthen interpersonal interactions, especially friendships through forgiveness), and the role of the adult mediator in children's verbal and/or physical conflicts.

Lastly, I would really enjoy delving into the significance of the 'culture of secrets' within children's friendship social circles, especially with reference to race, ethnicity, gender, language, and community. A purposeful starting interest might be children's secrets as a form of empowerment within their friendship groups. Actually, I would also like to explore the connections between language and secrets as a form of empowerment. Additionally, I would like to explore the types of secrets that children only keep for their friends and do not share with their peers. Finally, I would like to relate friendships with children's developing social personalities and why some children experience marginalized friendships, and others are locked out as outsiders.

Best Friends and the Games They Play

Meredith Gaskill

'Wherever Elementary School' (all personal and place names are fictitious) is a relatively small school in a rural county in the southeastern United States. The student body is made up of a little more than 500 students. I could not correctly estimate the socioeconomic make-up of the whole school, but within my classroom there was quite a diversity. There were clearly a few children who did not lack for much, and there were three or four who seemed to be living at the poverty level. Most were somewhere in the middle. There were more boys in this class than girls (13 to 8) which, as evidenced later, proved significant in their playground activities. The racial make-up of Wherever Elementary School is almost totally white; in my class, there was one black girl. I think this is an accurate representation of many of the classrooms in the school.

In my initial visit to Jennifer Leigh's third-grade classroom, I made two distinct observations of the playground friendships of these children. During the prefield visit, there was a large group of boys playing baseball. I began to wonder why these boys chose to play a team sport. How did they choose teams? Were the teams different everyday, or did they stay the same? Second, there was a group of three girls that I labeled as 'best friends.' Was this connotation one that I had assumed? Do third graders have any concept of what is involved in being a 'best friend,' or is it strictly an adult label and phenomenon? Is the friendship of these girls resilient, or does the bond that holds them together break at the slightest whim? These are the questions that I was trying to answer during my week of observation.

Boys and Team Sports

The first theme that I focused on dealt with the boys and team sports. During recess, the same group of seven or eight boys played kickball everyday.

On Day 1 there did not seem to be a dispute at all about who should be on each team. This contrasts with my initial prefield observation when I noted that boys spent the majority of their recess time 'picking teams' (Fieldnotes for Day 1).

On Day 2, after the boys had divided up and started playing, I asked Mark how the boys chose teams. He said, 'We have two captains who are "it" and they just pick the rest' (Fieldnotes for Day 2). I learned the next day that the captains are the first two boys who make it to the blacktop and yell, 'I'm a captain!' (Fieldnotes for Day 3). There were no hierarchies; the captains were simply the quickest to yell that they were the captains. Who each captain chose was the harder question to answer. Did each boy pick their own friends each day, or was it more random than that?

My hypothesis was that each day whoever became the captain would pick his own friends, and that the teams would stay the same throughout the week. However, I did not see this. On Day 3, Buck was a captain. 'I've got Russell,' he yelled, as his 'first pick.' Russell was a fourth grader from another class whose class happened to share the playground at the same time. Later, after the game, I asked Buck if he was friends with Russell. He said, 'No, I don't hardly know him.' I asked why then did he chose Russell first. Buck replied, 'Because he is in fourth grade and he is good [at kickball].' I asked him if he picked people just because they were good or because they were his friends. He said, 'Most of my friends are good, but I like to play with the fourth graders who are really good.' Based upon my observations, this group of children desired to win and their own competitiveness was the overriding motivator in choosing teams, superseding any notion of what I might have assumed as personal friendships.

Before I move on, I would like to note that there were never any girls involved in the kickball game. I asked one girl, Laurie, why she did not play kickball with the boys. She said, 'They are too mean.' I asked her if she thought the boys were always mean or just when they are playing kickball. She said, 'Mostly just outside. I have to sit with them in class and they are alright there.' I asked another girl, the lone black girl in the class, why she did not play kickball. She said she did not like it and she would rather do something else like jump rope or swing. According to Deegan (1993), gender is one of the strongest criteria for friendship with children at this age; my observations definitely back up this theory. I think this notion of girls not playing with boys was occurring in more ways than just in the kickball game. I did not have time to pursue this during the week.

Unravelling the Concept of 'Best Friends'

The most intriguing focus of my study was the concept of 'best friends.' In my initial prefield observation, I noted that there were 'three girls who . . . went to a bench and sat together in a huddle . . . These children were experiencing what it means to have a "best friend" or "best friends"' (Prefield Narrative

Write-up). They did not tell me that they were 'best friends.' Was this a term I created to label this triad or did they have any conception of their own of what it means to be a 'best friend'? On Day 1, I simply watched this threesome: Frankie, Judith, and Emily. My observations confirmed that they spent all their playground time solely with each other. They started out under the bleachers, then they went to a bench in the woods, and finally they went to the black-top where they took turns giving piggyback rides to each other (Fieldnotes for Day 1). On Day 2, Judith and Emily were absent. Frankie spent recess playing by herself, or standing next to me. I asked her why she was not doing anything and she said that she 'didn't have anybody to play with.'

Since I was not able to observe the girls, I took the opportunity to invest-igate other opinions that might exist about 'best friends' from other classmates. Moyra told me she had a best friend at her old school, but not at this school. She had moved to Wherever Elementary School at the beginning of the school year in August. She defined a 'best friend' as 'someone you like to play with more than anybody.' At Wherever Elementary School she said that she 'just has lots of friends, but no best friend.'

Porter and Adam are two boys who were a pair and always stuck together. I asked Porter if they were best friends. He said, 'Yes, can't you tell?' When I asked how I was supposed to be able to tell he said, 'I don't know, we just are — we always play together.'

On Day 3, Frankie, Judith, and Emily were back together again. They were sitting in the gazebo talking when I approached them. We began to talk and our conversation went as follows:

Int:	Do you all always play together?
All 3:	Yes
Int:	Why?
Frankie:	We like each other.
Judith:	We've known each other forever. [Forever turned out to be 'since first grade.']
Int:	Are you all best friends?
All 3:	Yes [in unison]
Int:	Why? What does that mean?
Frankie:	We only want to play with each other.
Int:	Can all three of you be best friends together, or is it hard to have two best friends?
Frankie:	It's not hard.
Emily:	We are all best friends.

The following day, Emily was absent. Frankie and Judith stuck together. I asked how they felt about Emily not being there. Frankie said, 'Yeah, we don't need her, we can still play with just each other.' Her comment seemed to con-tradict her earlier statement. She said it was not hard to have two best friends. Yet, now she says she does not need one of the two.

Based on everything I have seen and heard, I believe that children at this age have a very limited concept of 'best friend' as an interpersonal construct in the adult sense of how the concept might be used. In a journal entry from my own third-grade school experiences, I wrote that:

> A friend is someone who likes you. Not someone who calls you names and throws your toys. A best friend is someone who is gentle with you, who doesn't talk about you behind your back, and someone who will play with you.

To children of this age a 'best friend' is someone who will play with them. It is someone who shares a history, even a short history, with themselves. Their 'best friend' is someone who likes to play the games that they like to play. Deegan (1993) believes that children's friendships are built on consonance; they are built on encounter, togetherness, sharing, and niceness. Frankie, Judith, and Emily have all known each other for two years. They share many of the same interests and it is convenient for them to be friends. I think these friendships are probably not very resilient and as interests among the friends change, the 'best friend' ties may not last. Drawing from my own experience, I can remember my 'best friend' in third grade, called Virginia Stubbs. In fourth grade we were not in the same class and we did not get to play together, and the friendship ended.

I found my research on 'best friends' extremely interesting. As a future teacher, I believe this kind of research will be beneficial for me. Anything that allows us to get into the mind of a child can only help us become more effective teachers. In the future, I hope I can continue to observe and research this theme. I would love to focus more on male 'best friends.' Is their definition different from that of females? Are there more female or more male 'best friends'? Are there any male/female 'best friends' at this age? I hope that when I get into my own classroom that I can work with my findings from this action research project. It should be different when I know the children at a more personal and intimate level as their classroom teacher than as an intruder in their classroom for one week.

An Example of an E-mail Communication Sent by the Writer in Response to a Question from Meredith Gaskill

Date: Wed, 17 May 95 12:50:37 EDT From: JIM DEEGAN
<JDEEGAN-UGA.CC.UGA.EDU> Subject: Re: playground
project To: Meredith Gaskill
<mgaskill-?MOE.COE.UGA.EDU>

Meredith: Delighted that someone else is sharing my enthusiasm for the topic. The concept of 'best friends' is, as you correctly point out, an intriguing one. It changes over the developmental lifespan and means different things to different people at different times. So follow up as much as you can on this intriguing topic. Also check for inconsistencies — do kids have different 'best friends' from day to day. Labeling can often happen when adults impose their ways of looking at the world on kids. Simply, children might not use the same adult register when they express the realities of their social worlds. And then on the other hand, they might have a very sophisticated understanding of friendships, and this would be really interesting stuff. So — try and deconstruct the notion.

'Disconfirming evidence' is something that doesn't fit with everything else. Nine kids that you spoke to said that everyone is a best friend in their class and the 10th kid that you spoke to said that he doesn't have any best friends and, further, that there are no best friends in the class. This could be 'disconfirming evidence.' It is certainly worth chasing up. Sometimes disconfirming evidence helps you prove your point. It can become the exception that proves the rule. Whatever conclusions you arrive at, remember that it is ethical to indicate what didn't fit in, when, where, why, and how (if possible).

Keep up the good work. Sounds promising. And stay in contact. JDEEGAN

Chapter 8

Frontiers and Futures: Linking Theory, Research and Practice and the Challenge of Educational Reform

> Perhaps, I tell myself, we must be taught by parents, friends, or bad luck — what it means to be human. (Cole, 1993, p. 84)

My concern throughout the preceding chapters was not to present a grandiose schema of interrelated thematic trajectories on children's friendships in culturally diverse classrooms. Neither was it an attempt to engage in debunking the inherited research context of any given discipline. Instead, it was an attempt to explicate certain linking patterns that are evident in the theory, research, and pedagogy of children's friendships across disciplinary boundaries, and to demonstrate the usefulness of seeking linkages that often remain covert, or neglected, as a result of hidebound academic traditions and divisions. A more comprehensive fusing of the 'tensions' between and among all relevant disciplines is beyond the scope of this book.

Having addressed the etiological (see Chapter 2), operational (see Chapter 3), and applied (see Chapters 4, 5, 6, and 7) 'interrogatives' of children's friendships which were stated at the outset (see Chapter 1), the parting question becomes: What 'resonances' are sparked by my attempts to link the theory, research, and pedagogy of 'promising' nonsynchronous children's friendships in culturally diverse classrooms? This book sparks the following four distinct resonances:

1. Children's friendships as caring;
2. Children's friendships as motivational contexts for learning;
3. Children's friendships as meaningful explanatory frameworks for everyday living; and
4. Children's friendships as diffusive and generative phenomena.

These resonances will be discussed as frontiers and potential trajectories for future research, theory, and pedagogy on children's friendships.

Whenever the pronoun 'we' is used in the discussion, it embraces all those who believe in responsible advocacy for children's meaningful social lives in classrooms and schools, including university faculty, cooperating teachers, student teachers, school administrators, classroom teachers, parents, and, especially, children themselves. Being closest to the action on a daily basis privileges classroom teachers as potentially key pivotal advocates and researchers of the classroom processes of affect, inclusion, and power, and the integral themes and strands of the relationships that matter most to children. In the end, however, the fruits of our work will not be seen necessarily in the fervor of our advocacy, or the sophistication of our research designs, but rather in the extent to which we help children raise their own perspectives on their social lives in today's increasingly culturally diverse classrooms.

Children's Friendships as Caring

Noddings (1992) suggests a number of starting points for organizing education around salient themes of 'caring.' She situates friendships in her discussion of 'caring and the inner circle,' in which 'one person A, the carer, cares for another B, and B recognizes that A cares for B' (p. 91). In this conceptualization, it behooves teachers to respect the equality of relations that underpins children's friendships. I would like to suggest a variant of Noddings' (1992) approach for what we must do if we are to firmly establish children's friendships in emergent educational renewal and development. Noddings' (1992) suggestions are elaborated here with reference to Troyna and Hatcher's (1992) suggestions for what we can do when attempting to combine harmony and conflict, on the one hand, and equality and dominance, on the other, in children's friendships in culturally diverse classrooms and schools.

Be Firm in our Resolve about the Importance of Children's Friendships

The wonder of friendships is that they can be found everywhere. The obverse holds equally true. There is little wonder in phenomena that are pervasive. Our claims for the importance of children's friendships need to be grounded in helping children raise perspectives on their own 'real' world everyday social lives in classrooms and schools. After Cole's (1993) writings on the 'responsibility to respond' to friendships, we need to advocate clear and firm school policies to deal with children's friendships related to unique and contingent 'mixes' of race, gender, class, disability, community, and other sociocultural phenomena in our local education settings.

Develop Motivational Contexts for Children's Friendships

(a) Keep friends together (by mutual consent) over a number of years.
(b) Keep friends together where possible in regular and multi-age classroom cohorts.

(c) Keep friends in the same building for considerable periods of time.
(d) Help children to think about school as a conducive context for *their* friendships.
(e) Legitimize time spent in building relations of care and trust.
(f) Keep vigilant about potential threats to the motivational contexts of children's friendships posed by stereotyping, name-calling, and exclusionary practices.

Relax the Impulse to Control Children's Friendships

(a) Give children more responsibility to exercise judgment about their friendships.
(b) Encourage children to explore the everyday meanings of their friendships with each other.
(c) Examine the things that matter most to children in their friendships.
(d) Develop management approaches that are conducive for active social responsibility.
(e) Keep a judicious balance between the specter of litigation which often results in teachers calling for restrictions on children's playground lives, and the compelling research on the developmental significance of children's play.

Encourage Ways of Embedding Friendships in Action-based Classroom Conversations

(a) Give at least part of the day to themes that matter most to children, and this will, invariably, include some variant on friendships.
(b) Help children to practice caring and treating each other ethically.
(c) Help children to understand how groups and individuals can be potentially harmonious and conflictual. Help them to learn to be on 'both sides.'
(d) Help children to conceptualize friendships, broadly, by encouraging them to develop care for their friends' engaging ideas, including those that might be deeply rooted in distinctive cultural routines, rituals, and practices.

Promote the Idea that Friendships Show Moral Strength and Courage

(a) Recognize qualities of loyalty and trust that friends share with each other.
(b) Develop the idea of mutuality in friendships, and keep searching for the special ways that friends can bring out the best in each other.

(c)   Honor situations when friends stand up for each other's legitimate interests and concerns.

(d)   Promote the efforts of friends who prevent other friends from behaving in ethically or morally inappropriate ways.

(e)   Help raise children's voices on their own friendships, including the judicious raising of the immediate challenges of friendships in any given classroom situation.

Children's Friendships as Learning

It is generally agreed that children's friendships provide valuable contexts for learning about sharing and social participation, dealing with confusions, concerns, fears, and conflicts in children's lives, and resisting and challenging adult rules and authority (see Corsaro and Eder, 1990). We are still, however, only beginning to gather insights about children's perspectives on their own friendship routines, rituals, activities, concerns, and values, and how these meanings become embedded in their peer cultures.

While much work remains to be done, the stories of Jonathan, Lena, and Donna in Chapter 4, and other stories reported in this book, indicate the importance of examining children's perspectives on their own friendships as motivational contexts for learning in culturally diverse classrooms. These children's friendship-negotiating attempts showed that, in most cases, they were as socially 'promising' as their classmates and that dissonant contexts were not absolute, but negotiable ones. They provide strong evidence for the robustness of children and childhood in the present cultures of classrooms and schools. This is not intended as the end of the matter, but rather as the legitimate starting point. In this regard, the findings in the present study overlap with some of the earlier research on the nonsynchronous effects of dissonance on children's friendships (Clement, Eisenhart, and Harding, 1979; Grant, 1984; Schofield, 1981, 1982; Sleeter and Grant, 1986). Rosenberg (1975) put it succinctly when he pointed out that the 'dissonant context may have some effects that are positive and others that are negative' (p. 114).

Learning to seize the positive effects of children's friendships is a critical challenge. It is imperative for teachers to recognize when some children are making sincere attempts to cultivate their friendships in the face of severe life-situational dissonances. In classrooms where teachers understand that some children are carrying special challenges related to life-situational dissonances, teachers have the potential to facilitate productive social relationships. On the other hand, where there is a lack of understanding of the special needs of children from dissonant contexts, there is the danger that evaluations of the efforts of children like Jonathan, Lena, and Donna could be simplistically based on what are often negative outcomes, rather than on their thwarted attempts to effectively negotiate their friendships.

Children's Friendships and Meaningful Explanatory Frameworks for Everyday Living

Given 'current tendencies in reformist curriculum and educational discourses to treat minorities as homogeneous or undifferentiated groups' (McCarthy, 1990, p. 135), it is suggested that teachers should be wary of making unwarranted generalizations about what they perceive as examples of antisocial behavior rooted in race, ethnicity, gender, socioeconomic statues, or any other variable. As Goodenough (1987) has cautioned, aggregate analyses help account for stereotypical processes in culture, but 'they should not lure us into the false expedient of forgetting to look for individual and small group differences' (p. 96). By drawing attention to the consonant and dissonant features of children's friendships, this book has attempted to refine existing theoretical and conceptual foci on children's friendships in culturally diverse classrooms. If our understanding of children's friendships in culturally diverse classrooms is to accurately reflect what is really going on there, then we cannot afford to neglect the experiences of children like Jonathan, Lena, and Donna. Further investigations should be directed at investigating how children in other culturally diverse settings negotiate the unique and contingent 'mixes' of life-situational factors in the everyday world of their friendships.

The extant literature suggests that children's friendships in culturally diverse classrooms have interactive outcomes and are systematically contradictory or nonsynchronous. What is especially significant is that these outcomes can potentially lead to an increase or decrease in the effects of race, class, gender, or any other sociocultural variable, in local education settings.

There is a comprehensive supply of multicultural approaches that address the topic of children's social relationships in culturally diverse contexts on the market. I have attempted to eschew the approach that begins with arbitrary and convenient so-called multicultural 'packages' or 'hold-all' textbooks in favor of one that advocates that teachers need to make children's friendships a focus for their own action research projects. The outcome of these projects could potentially help teachers derive meaningful adaptations, modifications, and translations from the corpus of culturally sensitive learning and teaching strategies that are currently available on the market.

I would like to conclude this section by suggesting an ameliorative approach for addressing some general themes and strands in the literature on friendships and culturally sensitive pedagogies. These suggestions combine anti-racist curriculum (Troyna and Hatcher, 1992), anti-bias curriculum (Derman-Sparks and ABC Task Force, 1989), developmental approaches (Ramsey, 1987), broad-based multicultural approaches (Tiedt and Tiedt, 1995; York, 1991), personal and social education curriculum (Needham, 1994); and social reconstructionist approaches (Grant and Sleeter, 1989). The thrust of the suggestions combine the activism of anti-racist approaches which address structural inequities with the optimism of multicultural approaches which address a range of human relations needs in children's lives. Although the suggestions are presented heuristically, in essence, they are integrally related and holistic. Additionally, the suggestions that follow have a broad application across the whole gamut of children's social learning in culturally diverse classrooms. The teacher's role is pivotal in helping seal the friendship ties that exist in individual educational settings.

'The first [theme] is the centrality of the child' (Troyna and Hatcher, 1992, p. 201). Interactional themes and common-sense ideologies evident in the ethnographic literature in this book include the salience of linking children's own socially constructed ties with facilitative structural policies in culturally diverse schools. One of the strengths of teaching for diversity is that it can potentially become an affirmation of quality learning and teaching across the curriculum. Topics that could be interactively developed in culturally diverse classrooms to stimulate action-based conversations on children's interactional themes and ideologies include:

1. Integrating children's friendship interests as useful explanatory frameworks in everyday learning across the curriculum.
2. Celebrating children's playground lives as lenses for addressing what matters most to children.
3. Giving voice to different children's friendships by empowering children through language and talking with children about differences.
4. Actively listening to more than one side to a story.
5. Avoiding grouping that defines children as 'inferior' or reflects stereotyping.

The second theme is the need to help children develop understandings of equality and justice in their lives. Troyna and Hatcher (1992) call for programs that address 'both the dynamic towards equality and harmony and dominance and conflict' in children's friendships (p. 48). They further argued that all children derive a unique and contingent concept of race which is refashioned into common sense through practical experience, and has implications for dominance and equality in children's interactions and relationships with other children. Topics that could be interactively developed in culturally diverse classrooms to stimulate understandings of equality include:

1. Using creative conflict resolution rather than 'winner' takes all strategies.
2. Modeling that there is more than one 'right' cultural practice.
3. Providing children with meaningful choices in their learning.
4. Recognizing individual and democratic decision making.
5. Making connections between home, school, and community.
6. Paying attention to the reality of diverse families.
7. Making connections between children's 'own' everyday experiences and broader social issues.

A third point concerns the existence of racism, classism, and sexism in children's lives. Features of these practices can be public, for example, sloganizing on walls, t-shirts, baseball caps, insignia or badges. These features often transgress children's school and community norms and need to be readily handled by legitimate authorities. Other forms can be difficult to detect, for example, derogatory name-calling in a distant area of the playground, verbal and physical threats in school rest rooms, quiet ridicule of individual for a cultural preference in food. Topics that could be interactively developed in culturally diverse classrooms to stimulate understandings of these phenomena include:

1. Avoiding 'assaultive' discussions of race, gender, class, or other sociocultural phenomena where commonalities in diversity are sacrificed to differences. Keep a balance between commonalities and differences.
2. Collaborative checking between and among friends for racist, sexist, and classist language in reading materials.
3. Challenging actual instances of stereotyping through culturally responsive strategies.
4. Self-checking to see what messages visuals are giving to students about friendships.
5. Correcting negative images on television, in magazines, and in comics.
6. Displaying diversity in language, race, ethnicity, gender, class, disability and community materials and resources, notwithstanding a display of local children's friendships in prominent locations.

Children's Friendships as Diffusive and Generative Phenomena

Given the mounting impetus for private and religious schools, and the current popular debate on school choice (Elam, Rose, and Gallup, 1992), developments which could potentially affect many children on the bases of stereotypical sociocultural patterns of inclusion and exclusion in institutional settings, a study of the role that friendships play in children's everyday understandings of contingent mixes of sociocultural phenomena in majority-white elementary schools is propitious. It is especially true in the southern United States, for example, where historically 'schools of choice' were used to guarantee the continuation of a dual school system, and where recently there was renewed public controversy concerning attempts to resurrect a 1960s Georgia law providing for a school voucher system (see, for example, *The Atlanta Constitution and Journal*, October, 1993). Much of the current popular and academic debate has been heavily cast in broadly defined 'institutional' and 'ideological' (Fowler, 1991) terms, with little sense of how children might be affected by school choice.

It is argued here that understanding more about how children are experiencing a variety of sociocultural phenomena in their social lives in public and private schools should be embedded in the current debate on the social processes of affect, notably friendships, inclusion, and power in majority-white public, private, and religious schools. Sleeter (1993) wrote on the issue of how white teachers construct race, arguing that 'a predominantly white teaching force in a racist and multicultural society is not good for anyone, if we wish to reverse rather than reproduce racism' (p. 157). Research directed at examining how children in predominantly white schools construct meanings of race and other sociocultural phenomena needs to be examined if we are interested in finding out if racism is reproducing or reversing in private schools. How children's friendships play out in these increasingly popular educational contexts is integrally significant in this research.

Outward and Upward

The examples of the voices that can be heard in the previous chapters call to heart and mind some of the other voices that have been struggling to be heard in the din of popular and academic protests surrounding cultural diversity in contemporary society. Mindful of Van Maanen's (1988) advice to consider 'the fullness of the empty sign' (p. 26), it is worth remembering that within these stories lie the voices of those still waiting to be heard. For some, their contexts have yet to be examined, their perspectives heard, and their voices raised from whispers in the academic and popular protest. Casting 'harsh light' and 'soft focus', after Peacock's (1986) photographic metaphors, on the paradoxical challenges of children struggling to get along despite the odds is unfinished work in research, theory, and pedagogy on children's friendships in educational discourse. Not forgetting to listen for the whispered voices of children's 'promising' friendships in culturally diverse contexts is also unfinished work. This book suggests some learning and teaching opportunities that we might develop 'outward and upward' when we are among children's friendships in culturally diverse classrooms.

References

Aboud, F. (1988) *Children and Prejudice*, New York, Blackwell.

Adler, P.A. and Adler, P. (1987) *Membership Roles in Field Research*, Newbury, California, Sage.

Allan, D. (1952) *The Philosophy of Aristotle*, New York, Oxford University Press.

Allexsaht-Snider, M., Deegan, J.G., and White, C.S. (1995) 'Educational renewal in an alternative teacher education program: Evolution of a school-university partnership', *Teaching and Teacher Education*, **2**, 5, pp. 1–12.

Allport, G.A. (1928) 'A test for ascendance-submission', *Journal of Abnormal Psychology*, **23**, pp. 118–36.

Allport, G. (1954) *The Nature of Prejudice*, New York, Anchor.

Ambert, A.M. (1986) 'Sociology of sociology: The place of children in North American sociology', *Sociological Studies of Child Development*, **1**, pp. 3–31.

Apple, M. and Weiss, L. (1983) *Ideology and Practice in Schooling*, Philadelphia, Temple University Press.

Aries, P. (1962) *Centuries of Childhood*, London, Jonathan Cape.

Asher, S.R. and Gottman, J.M. (eds) (1981) *The Development of Children's Friendships*, New York, Cambridge University Press.

Assnick, B.B. (1993) 'An open letter to Suzanne de Castell and Tom Walker', *Anthropology and Education Quarterly*, **24**, 3, pp. 249–55.

Atkinson, P. (1980) *Writing Ethnography*, Mimeo.

Atkinson, P. (1990) *The Ethnographic Imagination: Textual Constructions of Reality*, London, Routledge.

Atwell, N. (1987) *In the Middle*, Portsmouth, New Hampshire, Heinemann.

Bales, R.F. (1970) *Personality and Interpersonal Relations*, New York, Holt, Rinehart and Winston.

Berndt, T.J. (1981) 'Relations between social cognition, nonsocial cognition, and social behavior: The case of friendship', in Flavell, J.H. and Ross, L. (eds) *Social Cognitive Development*, Cambridge, Cambridge University Press.

Berndt, T.J. (1983) 'Social cognition, social behavior, and children's friendships', in Higgins, E.T., Ruble, D.N., and Hartup, W.W. (eds) *Social Cognition and Social Development: A Sociocultural Perspective*, Cambridge, Cambridge University Press.

Bernstein, B. (1960) 'Language and social class', *British Journal of Sociology*, **2**, pp. 217–76.

BERREMAN, G.D. (1962) 'Behind many masks: Ethnography and impression management in a Himalayan village', *Society for Applied Anthropology, Monograph 4*, pp. 4–24.

BIGELOW, B.J. (1977) 'Children's friendship expectations: A cognitive-developmental study', *Child Development*, **48**, pp. 246–53.

BIGELOW, B. and LaGAIPA, J. (1975) 'Children's written description of friendship: A multidimensional analysis', *Developmental Psychology*, **11**, pp. 857–8.

BISSEX, G. and BULLOCK, R. (eds) (1987) *Seeing for Ourselves: Case-Study Research by Teachers of Writing*, Portsmouth, New Hampshire, Heinemann.

BLUMER, H. (1954) 'What is wrong with social theory?', *American Sociological Review*, **19**, pp. 3–10.

BLUMER, H. (1969) *Symbolic Interactionism*, Englewood Cliffs, New Jersey, Prentice-Hall.

BLUMER, H. (1976) 'Sociological implications of the thought of G.H. Mead', in COSIN, B.R. (ed.) *School and Society*, London, Routledge and Kegan Paul.

BOGDAN, R.C. and BIKLEN, S.K. (1982) *Qualitative Research for Education: An Introduction to Theory and Methods*, Boston, Allyn and Bacon.

BOON, J. (1982) *Other Tribes, Other Scribes: Symbolic Anthropology in the Comparative Study of Cultures, Histories, Religions, and Texts*, Cambridge, Cambridge University Press.

BOOSTROM, R. (1994) 'A curriculum of caring', *Curriculum Studies*, **26**, 1, pp. 97–114.

BOTT, H. (1934) 'Personality development in young children', *University of Toronto Studies, Child Development Series*, **1**, 2.

BOURDIEU, P. and PASSERON, J.C. (1977) *Reproduction in Education, Society, and Culture*, London, Sage.

BOWLES, S. and GINTIS, H. (1976) *Schooling in Capitalist America*, London, Routledge and Kegan Paul.

BRICE HEATH, S. (1993) 'The madness(es) of reading and writing ethnography', *Anthropology and Education Quarterly*, **24**, 3, pp. 256–68.

BROWN, R.H. (1989) *A Poetic for Sociology: Towards a Logic of Discovery for Human Sciences*, Chicago, University of Chicago Press.

BRUNER, J. (1986) *Actual Minds, Possible Worlds*, Cambridge, Massachusetts, Harvard University Press.

BRYCE, J. (1916) *The American Commonwealth*, New York, Macmillan.

BULMER, M. (1984) *The Chicago School of Sociology: Institutionalization, Diversity and the Rise of Sociological Research*, Chicago, University of Chicago Press.

CARRINGTON, B. and SHORT, G. (1992) 'Researching "race" in the all-white primary school: The ethics of curriculum development', in LEICESTER, M. and TAYLOR, M. (eds) *Ethics, Ethnicity, and Education*, London, Kogan Page.

CAUDILL, W. (1958) *The Psychiatric Hospital as a Small Society*, Cambridge, Massachusetts, Cambridge University Press.

CHANCE, P. and FISCHMAN, J. (1987) 'The magic of childhood', *Psychology Today*, **21**, 5, pp. 49–58.

CLARK, K. and CLARK, M. (1947) 'Racial identification and preference in negro children', in NEWCOMB, T.M. and HARTLEY, E.L. (eds) *Readings in Social Psychology*, New York, Holt, Rinehart and Winston.

CLEMENT, D., EISENHART, M. and HARDING, D. (1979) 'The veneer of harmony: Social-race relations in a southern desegregated school', in RIST, R.C. (ed.) *Desegregated Schools: Appraisals of an American Experiment*, New York, Academic Press.

COCHRAN-SMITH, M. (1991) 'Reinventing student teaching', *Journal of Teacher Education*, **2**, 2, pp. 104–111.

COHEN, A.P. (1985) *The Symbolic Construction of Community*, London, Tavistock.

COHEN, J. (1977) 'Sources of peer homogeneity', *Sociology of Education*, **50**, pp. 227–41.

COLE, D. (1993) 'Responsibility to respond: What one friend owes another', *Utne Reader*, (September/October), p. 84.

COLEMAN, J.S. (1961) 'Comment on three "climate of opinion" studies', *Public Opinion Quarterly*, **25**, 4, pp. 607–10.

CONNELLY, M.P. and CLANDININ, D.J. (June/July, 1990) 'Stories of experience and narrative inquiry', *Educational Researcher*, pp. 2–14.

COOLEY, C.H. (1902) *Human Nature and Social Order*, New York, Scribner.

CORSARO, W.A. (1981) 'Friendship in the nursery school: Social organization in a peer environment', in ASHER, S.R. and GOTTMAN, J.M. (eds) *The Development of Children's Friendships*, New York, Cambridge University Press, pp. 207–41.

CORSARO, W.A. (1985) *Friendship and Peer Culture in the Early Years*, Norwood, New Jersey, Ablex.

CORSARO, W.A. (1994) 'Discussion, debate, and friendship processes: Peer discourse in the US and Italian nursery schools', *Sociology of Education*, **67**, pp. 1–26.

CORSARO, W.A. and EDER, D. (1990) 'Children's peer cultures', *Annual Review of Sociology*, **16**, pp. 197–220.

CORSARO, W.A. and RIZZO, T.A. (1988) ' "Discussions" and friendship: Socialization processes in the peer culture of Italian nursery school children', *American Sociological Review*, **53**, pp. 879–94.

CRICK, M. (1976) *Explorations in Language and Meaning*, London, Malaby Press.

CRISSWELL, J.H. (1939) 'A sociometric study of race cleavage in the classroom', *Archives of Psychology*, **235**.

DAMICO, S.B. (1974) 'The relation of clique membership to achievement, self-concept, social acceptance, and school attitude', *Dissertation Abstracts International*, **35**, 2, p. 717.

DAMON, W. (1983) 'The nature of social cognitive change in the developing child', in OVERTON, W.F. (ed.) *The Relationship between Social and Cognitive Development*, Hillsdale, New Jersey, Erlbaum.

DAVEY, A. (1983) *Learning to be Prejudiced*, London, Arnold.

References

DAVIES, B. (1982) *Life in the Classroom and Playground: The Accounts of Primary School Children*, London, Routledge.

DAVIES, B. (1984) 'Friends and fights', in HAMMERSLEY, M. and WOODS, P. (eds) *Life in Schools: The Sociology of Pupil Cultures*, Milton Keynes, Open University Press, pp. 255–69.

DEEGAN, J.G. (1990) 'Children's friendships in a fifth-grade culturally diverse classroom.' Unpublished doctoral dissertation, The University of Georgia, Athens.

DEEGAN, J.G. (1992) 'Understanding vulnerable friendships in fifth-grade culturally diverse classrooms', *Middle School Journal*, **23**, 4, pp. 20–5.

DEEGAN, J.G. (1993) 'Children's friendships in culturally diverse classrooms', *Journal of Research in Childhood Education*, **7**, 2, pp. 91–101.

DEEGAN, J.G. (1995) 'The friendly cultural stranger as self-critical reflexive narrator', *Anthropology and Education Quarterly*, **26**, 3, pp. 349–57.

DEEGAN, J.G. and PELLEGRINI, A.D. (1994) 'Play and trajectories for social origins of cognition', in BOGUE, R. and SPARIOSU, M. (eds) *The Play of the Self*, New York, SUNY Press.

DENSCOMBE, M., SZULC, H., PATRICK, C. and WOOD, A. (1986) 'Ethnicity and friendship: The contrast between sociometric research and fieldwork observation in primary school classrooms', *British Educational Research Journal*, **12**, 3, pp. 221–35.

DENZIN, N.K. (1977) *Childhood Socialization*, San Francisco, Jossey-Bass.

DERMAN-SPARKS, L. and ABC TASK FORCE (1989) *Anti-Bias Curriculum: Tools for Empowering Young Children*, Washington, DC, NAEYC.

DION, K. and BERSCHEID, E. (1974) 'Physical attraction and peer perception among children', *Sociometry*, **37**, pp. 1–12.

DUNDES, A. (1971) 'Folk ideas as units of worldview', in PAREDRES, A. and BAUMAN, R. (eds) *Toward New Perspectives in Folklore*, Austin, University of Texas Press.

DUNN, L. (1987) *Bilingual Hispanic Children on the US Mainland: A Review of Research on their Cognitive, Linguistic, and Scholastic Development*, Circle Pines, Minnesota, American Guidance Service.

DURKHEIM, E. and MAUS, M. (1966 [1903]) 'Dequelques formes primitives de classifications', in MAUS, M. (ed.) *Oeuvres*, **2**, Paris, Editions de Minuit.

EBUTT, D. and PARTINGTON, D. (1982) 'Self-monitoring by teachers', in BOLAM, R. (ed.) *School-Focused In-Service Training*, London, Heinemann.

EDGERTON, S.H. (1993) 'Toni Morrison teaching the interminable', in McCARTHY, C. and CRITCHLOW, W. (eds) *Race Identity and Representation in Education*, London, Routledge.

ELAM, S., ROSE, L. and GALLUP, A. (1992) 'The 24th annual Gallup/Phi Delta Kappa poll of the public attitudes toward the public schools', *Phi Delta Kappa*, **74**, 1, pp. 41–53.

EPSTEIN, J.L. (1983) 'Friends among students in schools: Environmental and developmental factors', in EPSTEIN, J.L. and KARWEIT, N. (eds) *Friends in School: Patterns of Selection and Influence in Secondary Schools*, New York, Academic Press.

ERICKSON, F. (1984) 'What makes school ethnography "Ethnographic"?', *Anthropology and Education Quarterly*, **15**, 1, pp. 51–6.

FINE, G.A. (1980) 'The natural history of preadolescent friendship groups', in FOOT, H., CHAPMAN, A., and SMITH, J. (eds) *Friendship and Social Relations in Children*, New York, Wiley.

FINE, G.A. (1981) 'Friends and impression management, and preadolescent behavior', in ASHER, S.R. and GOTTMAN, J.M. (eds) *The Development of Children's Friendships*, New York, Cambridge University Press.

FINE, G.A. (1987) *With the Boys: Little League Baseball and Preadolescent Culture*, Chicago, Chicago University Press.

FINE, G.A. (1993) 'Ten lies of ethnography: Moral dilemmas of field research', *Journal of Contemporary Ethnography*, **22**, 3, pp. 267–95.

FINE, G.A. and SANDSTROM, K.L. (1988) *Knowing Children: Participant Observation with Minors*, Beverly Hills, Sage.

FLORIO-RUANE, S. (1990) 'Creating your own case study', *Teacher Education Quarterly*, **17**, 1, pp. 29–41.

FORSTER, E.M. (1927) *Aspects of the Novel*, London, Edward Arnold.

FOWLER, F.C. (1991) 'The shocking ideological integrity of Chubb and Moe', *Journal of Education*, **173**, 3.

GIDDENS, A. (1976) *The New Rules of Sociological Method*, London, Hutchinson.

GIDDENS, A.P. (1984) *The Constitution of Society: Outline of the Theory of Structuration*, Berkeley, University of California Press.

GIDDENS, A. (1985) *The Constitution of Society*, Cambridge, Polity Press.

GILLBORN, G. (1995, April) 'Racism, modernity, and schooling: New directions in antiracist theory and practice.' Paper presented at the annual meeting of the American Educational Research Association, San Francisco.

GINSBERG, D., GOTTMAN, J.M. and PARKER, J. (1986) 'The importance of friendship', in GOTTMAN, J.M. and PARKER, J.G. (eds) *Conversations of Friends: Speculations on Affective Development*, London, Cambridge University Press.

GLASER, B.G. and STRAUSS, A.L. (1967) *The Discovery of Grounded Theory: Strategies for Qualitative Research*, Chicago, Aldine.

GOETZ, J.P. and LeCOMPTE, M.D. (1984) *Ethnography and Qualitative Design in Educational Research*, New York, Academic Press.

GOFFMAN, E. (1959) *The Presentation of Self*, Garden City, New York, Doubleday.

GOODENOUGH, W.H. (1987) 'Multiculturalism as the normal experience', in EDDY, E.M. and PARTRIDGE, W.L. (eds) *Applied Anthropology in America*, New York, Columbia University Press.

GOODLAD, J.I. (1994) *Educational Renewal: Better Teachers, Better Schools*, San Francisco, Jossey-Bass.

GOODWIN, M.H. (1985) 'The serious side of jump rope: Conversational practices and social organization in the frame of play', *Journal of American Folklore*, **98**, pp. 315–30.

GOSWAMI, D. and STILLMAN, P. (eds) (1987) *Reclaiming the Classroom: Teacher Research as an Agency for Change*, Portsmouth, New Hampshire, Heinemann/Boynton-Cook.

References

GRAMSCI, A. (1977) *Selections from Political Writings, 1910–20* (ed. Q. Hoare), London, Lawrence and Wishart.

GRANT, C.A. and SLEETER, C.E. (1989) *Turning on Learning: Five Approaches for Multicultural Teaching Plans for Race, Class, Gender, and Disability*, Columbus, Ohio, Merrill.

GRANT, L. (1981) 'Race, sex, and schooling: Social location of children's experiences in desegregated classrooms.' Unpublished doctoral dissertation, University of Michigan, Ann Arbor.

GRANT, L. (1984) 'Black females "place" in desegregated classrooms', *Sociology of Education*, **57**, pp. 98–111.

HALLINAN, M.T. (1980) 'Patterns of cliquing among youth', in FOOT, H., CHAPMAN, A. and SMITH, J. (eds) *Friendship and Social Relations in Children*, New York, Wiley.

HALLINAN, M.T. (1981) 'Recent advances in sociometry', in ASHER, S.R. and GOTTMAN, J.M. (eds) *The Development of Children's Friendships*, New York, Cambridge University Press.

HAMMERSLEY, M. (ed.) (1983) *The Ethnography of Schooling*, Driffield, Nafferton.

HAMMERSLEY, M. (1990) *Classroom Ethnography*, Milton Keynes, Open University Press.

HAMMERSLEY, M. and ATKINSON, P. (1983) *Ethnography: Principles in Practice*, London, Tavistock.

HAMMERSLEY, M. and HARGREAVES, A. (1983) *Curriculum Practice: Some Sociological Case Studies*, London, Falmer Press.

HARGREAVES, D.H. (1967) *Social Relations in the Secondary School*, London, Routledge and Kegan Paul.

HARGREAVES, D.H. (1978) 'Whatever happened to symbolic interactionism?', in BARTON, L. and MEIGHAN, R. (eds) *Sociological Interpretations of Education and Schooling*, Driffield, Nafferton.

HARRÉ, R. (1986) 'The step to social constructionism', in LIGHT, M.P. (ed.) *Children of Social Worlds; Development in a Social Context*, Cambridge, Harvard University Press.

HARTUP, W.W. (1983) 'Peer relations', in HETHERINGTON, E.M. (ed.) *Handbook of Child Psychology*, New York, Wiley.

HEWSTONE, M. and BROWN, R. (1986) 'Contact is not enough: An intergroup perspective on the contact hypothesis', in HEWSTONE, M. and BROWN, R. (eds) *Contact and Conflict in Intergroup Encounters*, New York, Blackwell.

HOROWITZ, E.I. (1965) 'Development of attitudes towards Negroes', in PROSCHANSKY, H. and SEIDENBERG, B. (eds) *Basic Studies in Social Psychology*, New York, Holt, Rinehart and Winston.

HUBBARD, R.S. and BROWN, B.M. (1993) *The Art of Classroom Inquiry: A Handbook for Teacher Researchers*, Portsmouth, New Hampshire, Heinemann.

HYMEL, S., WAGNER E. and BUTLER, L. (1990) 'Reputational bias: View from the peer group', in ASHER, S.R. and COIE, J. (eds) *Peer Rejection in Childhood*, New York, Cambridge University Press.

JACK, L.M. (1934) 'An experimental study of ascendant behavior in preschool children', *University of Iowa Studies in Child Welfare*, **9**, 3, pp. 9–65.

JACKSON, P.W. (1968) *Life in Classrooms*, New York, Holt, Rinehart and Winston.

JAMES, A. and PROUT, A. (eds) (1990) *Constructing and Reconstructing Childhood: Contemporary Issues in the Sociological Study of Childhood*, London, Falmer Press.

JENSEN, A. (1984) 'Political ideologies and educational research', *Phi Delta Kappa*, **65**, 7, p. 460.

JOHNSON, J.M. (1975) *Doing Field Research*, New York, Free Press.

KATRIEL, T. (1987) '"Bexibudim!": Ritualized sharing among Israeli children', *Language*, **16**, pp. 467–90.

KENNEDY, S. (1954) *The Klan Unmasked*, Boca Raton, Florida Atlantic University Press.

KIDDER, T. (1989) *Among School Children*, Boston, Houghton Mifflin.

KIERKEGAARD, S. (1965) *The Concept of Irony*, New York, Harper and Row.

KOCH, H.L. (1933) 'Popularity among preschool children: Some related factors and a technique for its measurement', *Child Development*, **4**, pp. 164–75.

KOZOL, J. (1967) *Death at an Early Age: The Destruction of the Hearts and Minds of Negro Children in the Boston Public Schools*, New York, New American Library.

KROEBER, A.L. and KLUCKHOHN, C. (1952) *Culture: A Critical Review of Concepts and Definitions*, Cambridge, Massachusetts, The Museum.

LANGWORTHY, R. (1959) 'Community status and influence in a high school', *American Sociological Review*, **24**, pp. 537–9.

LASKER, B. (1929) *Race Attitudes in Children*, New York, Greenwood Press.

LeCOMPTE, M.D. (1987) 'Bias in biography: Bias and subjectively in ethnographic research', *Anthropology and Education Quarterly*, **18**, pp. 43–52.

LEWIN, K. and LIPPITT, R. (1938) 'An experimental approach to the study of autocracy and democracy; A preliminary note', *Sociometry*, **1**, pp. 292–300.

LEWIN, K., LIPPITT, R. and WHITE, R.K. (1939) 'Patterns of aggressive behavior in experimentally created social climates', *Journal of Social Psychology*, **10**, pp. 271–99.

LIPPITT, R. and GOLD, M. (1959) 'Classroom social structure as a mental health problem', *Journal of Social Issues*, **15**, pp. 40–58.

LIPPITT, R. and WHITE, R.K. (1947) 'An experimental study of leadership and group life', in NEWCOMB, T.M. and HARTLEY, E.L. (eds) *Readings in Social Psychology*, New York, Holt, Rinehart.

LOPATE, P. (1993) 'What friends are for', *Utne Reader*, September/October, pp. 78–91.

MAC AN GHAILL, M. (1988) *Young, Gifted, and Black*, Philadelphia, Pennsylvania, Open University.

MALINOWSKI, B. (1922) *Argonauts of the Western Pacific*, London, Routledge and Kegan Paul.

References

MALINOWSKI, B. (1929) *The Sexual Life of Savages in Northwestern Melanesia*, London, Routledge.

MARSH, C.J. (1992) *Key Concepts for Understanding Curriculum*, London, Falmer Press.

MAYALL, B. (ed.) (1994) *Children's Childhoods: Observed and Experienced*, London, Falmer Press.

MCCALL, G.J. (1970) *Social Relationships*, Chicago, Aldine.

MCCANDLESS, B. and MARSHALL, H. (1957) 'A picture-sociometric technique for preschool children and its relation to teacher judgements of friendships', *Child Development*, **28**, pp. 139–48.

MCCARTHY, C. (1990) *Race and Curriculum: Social Inequality and Theories and Policies of Difference in Contemporary Research on Schooling*, London, Falmer Press.

MCCARTHY, C. and CRITCHLOW, W. (eds) (1993) *Race, Identity, and Representation in Education*, New York, Routledge.

MEAD, G.H. (1934) *Mind, Self and Society*, Chicago, University of Chicago Press.

MILES, R. (1988) 'Racialization', in CASHMORE, E. (ed.) *Dictionary of Race and Ethnic Relations*, London, Routledge.

MISHLER, E. (1979) ' "Won't you trade cookies with the popcorn?:" The talk of trades among six-year-olds', in GARNICA, O. and KING, M. (eds) *Language, Children, and Society: The Effects of Social Factors on Children's Learning to Communicate*, Elmsford, New York, Pergammon.

MONTGOMERY, L.M. (1944) *Anne of Green Gables*, New York, Henry Holt.

MORENO, J.L. (1934) *Who Shall Survive?: A New Approach to the Problem of Human Interrelations*, Washington, DC, Nervous and Mental Disease Publishing Company.

NEEDHAM, J. (1994) 'An approach to personal and social education in the primary school: Or how one city schoolteacher tried to make sense of her job', in POLLARD, A. and BOURNE, J. (eds) *Teaching and Learning in the Primary School*, London, Routledge.

NODDINGS, N. (1992) *The Challenge to Care: An Alternative Approach to Education*, New York, Teachers College Press.

OPIE, I. and OPIE, P. (1959) *The Lore and Language of Schoolchildren*, Oxford, Oxford University Press.

OPIE, I. and OPIE, P. (1969) *Children's Games in Street and Playground*, Oxford, Oxford University Press.

PAGE, M.L. (1936) 'The modification of ascendant behavior in preschool children', *University of Iowa Studies in Child Welfare*, **12**, pp. 7–69.

PALEY, V.P. (1989) *White Teacher*, Cambridge, Harvard University Press.

PARK, R. (1915) 'The city: Suggestions for the investigation of human behavior in an urban environment', *American Journal of Sociology*, **20**, pp. 577–612.

PATTON, M.Q. (1980) *Qualitative Research Methods*, Beverly Hills, Sage.

PEACOCK, J.L. (1986) *The Anthropological Lens: Harsh Light, Soft Focus*, Cambridge, Cambridge University Press.

PELLEGRINI, A.D. (1987) *Applied Child Study: A Developmental Approach*, Hillsdale, New Jersey, Erlbaum.

PELTO, P.J. and PELTO, G.H. (1973) 'Ethnography', in HONIGMANN, J.J. (ed.) *Handbook of Social and Cultural Anthropology*, Chicago, Rand McNally.

PESHKIN, A. (1986) *God's Choice: The Total World of a Fundamentalist Christian School*, Chicago, University of Chicago Press.

PESHKIN, A. (1988) 'In search of subjectivity — one's own', *Educational Researcher*, **17**, 1, pp. 17–21.

PETTIT, G., BASKI, A., DODGE, K. and COIE, J. (1990) 'The emergence of social dominance in young boys' playgroups: Developmental differences and behavioral correlates', *Developmental Psychology*, **26**, pp. 1017–25.

PIAGET, J. (1932) *Social Evolution and the New Education*, London, New Education Fellowship.

POWDERMAKER, H. (1966) *Stranger and Friend: The Way of an Anthropologist*, New York, W.W. Norton and Company.

PRITCHETT, V.S. (1967) *Dublin: A Portrait*, New York, Harper and Row.

POLLARD, A. (1985) *The Social World of the Primary School*, London, Holt, Rinehart and Winston.

POLLARD, A. (1990) 'Towards a sociology of learning in primary schools', *British Journal of Sociology of Education*, **11**, 3, pp. 241–56.

POLLARD, A. (1994) 'Towards a sociology of learning in primary schools', in POLLARD, A. and BOURNE, J. (eds) *Teaching and Learning in the Primary School*, London, Routledge.

POLLARD, A. and BOURNE, J. (eds) (1994) *Teaching and Learning in the Primary School*, London, Routledge.

POLLARD, A. and TANN, S. (1987) *Reflective Teaching in the Primary School*, London, Cassell.

RAMSEY, P.G. (1987) *Teaching and Learning in a Diverse World*, New York, Teachers College Press.

RENSHAW, P. (1981) 'The roots of peer interaction research: A historical analysis of the 1930s', in ASHER, S.R. and GOTTMAN, J.M. (eds) *The Development of Children's Friendships*, New York, Cambridge University Press.

RIZZO, T.A. (1989) *Friendship Development Among Children in School*, Norwood, New Jersey, Ablex.

RONAI, C.R. (1992) 'The reflexive self through narrative: A night in the life of an exotic dancer/researcher', in ELLIS, C.E. and FLAHERTY, M.G. (eds) *Investigating Subjectivity: Research on Lived Experience*, London, Sage.

ROSENBERG, M. (1975) 'The dissonant context and the adolescent self-concept', in DRAGASTIN, S. and ELDER, G. (eds) *Adolescence in the Life-Cycle: Psychological Change and Social Change*, Washington, DC, Hemisphere.

ROYCE, A.P. (1982) *Ethnic Identity: Strategies of Diversity*, Bloomington, Indiana University Press.

SCHOFIELD, J.W. (1981) 'Complementary and conflicting identities: Images and interaction in an interracial school', in ASHER, S.R. and GOTTMAN, J.M. (eds)

The Development of Children's Friendships, New York, Cambridge University Press.

SCHOFIELD, J.W. (1982) *Black and White in School: Trust, Tension, or Tolerance*, New York, Praeger.

SCHUTZ, A. (1970) *On Phenomenology and Social Relations*, Chicago, University of Chicago Press.

SELMAN, R.L. (1980) *The Growth of Interpersonal Understanding*, New York, Academic Press.

SHANTZ, C. (1983) 'Social cognition', in FLAVELL, J. and MARKHAM, E. (eds) *Handbook of Child Psychology, Cognitive Development*, **3**, New York, Wiley.

SHANTZ, C. (1987) 'Conflicts between children', *Child Development*, **58**, pp. 283–305.

SHERIF, M., HARVEY, O.J., WHITE, B.J., HOOD, W.R., and SHERIF, C.W. (1961) *Inter Group Conflict and Cooperation: The Robbers Cave Experiment*, Norman, University of Oklahoma Press.

SHILLING, C. (1992) 'Reconceptualizing structure and agency in the sociology of education: Structuration theory and schooling', *British Journal of Sociology of Education*, **13**, 1, pp. 68–87.

SHORT, G. (1993) 'Prejudice reduction in schools: The value of inter-racial contact', *British Journal of Sociology of Education*, **14**, 2, pp. 159–68.

SIMMEL, G. (1950) *The Sociology of Georg Simmel*, (ed. K.H. Wolff) Glencoe, Illinois, Free Press.

SLEETER, C.E. (1993) 'How white teachers construct race', in MCCARTHY, C. and CRITCHLOW, W. (eds) *Race, Identity, and Representation in Education*, New York, Routledge.

SLEETER, C.E. and GRANT, C.A. (1986) *After the School Bell Rings*, London, Falmer Press.

SLUCKIN, A. (1981) *Growing up in the Playground*, London, Routledge and Kegan Paul.

SPINDLER, G.D. (1982) 'The criteria for a good ethnography of schooling', in SPINDLER, G.D. (ed.) *Doing the Ethnography of Schooling: Educational Anthropology in Action*, New York, Holt, Rinehart and Winston.

SPRADLEY, J.P. and MCCURDY, D.W. (1975) *Anthropology: The Cultural Perspective*, New York, Wiley.

STRAUSS, A.L. (1987) *Qualitative Analysis for Social Scientists*, Cambridge.

SWADENER, B.B. and LUBECK, S. (eds) (1995) *Children and Families 'At Promise:' Deconstructing the Discourse of Risk*, Albany, SUNY.

TAYLOR, M.J. and HEGARTY, S. (1985) *The Best of Both Worlds . . . ?* Philadelphia, PA, NFER-Nelson.

TENNYSON, A. (1870) *The Poetical Works of Alfred Tennyson*, New York, Harper.

THRASHER, F. (1927) *The Gang: A Study of 1,313 Chicago Gangs*, Chicago, University of Chicago Press.

TIEDT, A.L. and TIEDT, I.M. (1995) *Multicultural Teaching: A Handbook of Activities, Information, and Resources*, London, Allyn and Bacon.

TRIPLETT, N. (1897) 'The dynamogenic factors in pacemaking and competition', *American Journal of Psychology*, **9**, pp. 507–33.

TROYNA, B. and HATCHER, R. (1992) *Racism in Children's Lives: A Study of Mainly-White Primary Schools*, London, Routledge.

TRUEBA, H. (1993) 'The ethnography of cultural diversity: Class, race and ethnicity in the fabric of American democracy', in DEEGAN, J.G. (ed.) *Cultural Diversity: Contexts, Perspectives, and Voice, (Proceedings of the Sixth Annual Conference on Qualitative Research in Education)*, Georgia, The University of Georgia, College of Education.

TYLOR, E.B. (1871) *Primitive Culture*, **1**, London, John Murray.

TWAIN, M. (1995 [1884]) *Adventures of Huckleberry Finn*, Berkeley, University of California Press.

VAN MANNEN, J. (1988) *Tales of the Field: On Writing Ethnography*, Chicago, University of Chicago Press.

WALKER, R. and WEIDEL, J. (1985) 'Using photographs in a discipline of words', in BURGESS, R. (ed.) *Field Methods in the Study of Education*, London, Falmer Press.

WHYTE, W.F. (1981) *Street Corner Society: The Social Structure of an Italian Slum*, Chicago, University of Chicago Press.

WOODS, P. (1990) *The Happiest Days?: How Pupils Cope with School*, London, Falmer Press.

YORK, S. (1991) *Roots and wings: Affirming Culture in Early Childhood Programs*, St. Paul, Minnesota, Redleaf Press.

YOUNISS, J. (1980) *Parents and Peers in Social Development: A Sullivan-Piaget Perspective*, Chicago, University of Chicago Press.

Index

Index